From Dawn to Daylight

Dawn Downey

From Dawn to Daylight
Essays

Dawn Downey

PATHLESS LAND PRESS
KANSAS CITY MO

From Dawn to Daylight
Copyright 2015 by Dawn Downey
All rights reserved.

Published 2015 by Pathless Land Press
Printed in the United States of America

ISBN 978-0-9963240-3-8

Cover design by Teresa Mandala
www.bella-designs.biz

Book design by Maureen Cutajar
www.gopublished.com

Author photo by Stephen Locke
www.stephenlocke.com

For Ben, my Vitamin B

Contents

PERSONALITY POWER FAILURE

Personality Power Failure	3
Transcending Tomatoes	4
Senior Moment	5
Mama's Lament	6
Center of Attention	7
The 2015 Dawn-mobile	8
Too Young for Old Age	9
Migraines, Why Me?	11
Pilgrimage	12
Speaking of My Life	14
Problem Solved	15
How to Give Advice	16
Mother's Day Schematic	17
Set in My Ways	18
Nirvana	19
Samsara	20
A Bovine Epiphany	21
A Second Bovine Epiphany	22
Faith	24
Ode to Dung Beetles	25
Show Pies	26
Porta-Potty Blues	27
City Girl Makes Peace with Nature: Lesson One	28
Multi-Lingual Flu	30

THE TIES THAT BIND

The Ties that Bind 35
The Day I Turned White 37
Post Office Paradox 39
Michelle's Face 40
Sunday Morning 41
Baby Powder 42
Little Lambs Choir 43
Christmas Adopt-a-Family 44
Best Friends 45
A Principled Woman 46
Love Letter to Donald Sterling 47
Chicagoland 48
Betrayed 50
Invisible Man 52
Basketball Moves 54
My New Office 55
Remembering Stef 56
Goodbye, Roger Ebert 58
A Pope for Thich Nhat Hanh 59
Pope Francis: The Latest Next Big Thing 60
Rare Birds 61
City Girl Makes Peace with Nature: Lesson Two 62
Racist Recipe 63
Seven Regrets 65
How Far Do You Need to Walk? 66

CLOSURE

Interrupted Conversation 71
Seven Fragrances I Miss 72
Old Photos 73
Forgive Me 75
Seven Wonders of the World 76
Chocolate Cake 77
Monsoon 78
Radiation Therapy Waiting Room 79

Corpse Pose	80
Candlelight Vigil	81
No Longer Mother	82
A Friend Lay Dying	84
Stephanie Bryan Died	85
Ten Thousand Things	86
Good Bones	87
Heads I'll Wake Up; Tails I Won't	89
Ancestor Games	90
Insomnia	91
Recycle	92
Boston Marathon	94
Cemetery Song	95
Dismantled	96
Closure	98
House on Fire	100
January 13, Five AM	102

AT HOME IN PARADISE

Gravity	107
Praise the Lord	109
History of the Dance	110
Morning Walk	111
Breakfast for Four at the Silent Retreat	112
In the Presence of Love	113
Winter Blues	114
Yard Work/Yard Play	115
Gardening vs. Yard Work	116
Swept Away	117
Inside the Flu	118
Less Worry. More Food.	119
California Redwoods	120
Gratitude for Ugly	121
Me, Myself, and I	122
Parkville Imagined	123
City Girl Makes Peace with Nature: Lesson Three	124

Avian Enchantment 125
Too-Tight Jeans 126
Washing Dishes at the Silent Retreat 128
What Do You Want? 129
So-Called Problems 130
Trite or Truth? 131
Alzheimer's Duet 132
At Home in Paradise 133

SAMPLE CHAPTERS

The Inheritance 137
Apple Pie for Two 147

Acknowledgements 153
About the Author 155

Personality Power Failure

Personality Power Failure

MY THERAPIST ASKED, "Are you under any stress?"

"Heck, no. Everything's wonder—. Wait. Yes." I slumped into the couch. "A friend bought ten copies of my book. Another bought five. They're writing reviews that are really moving. It's stressing me out. It's confusing. Sometimes I go blank."

"Positive affect disorder," he said.

Or was it positive affect deregulation? Or dehydration? Or deceleration?

"Negative comes in at a different voltage than positive. You're wired for negative. Too much good short-circuits the system."

I perked up. My brain loved to learn new things about itself. Cause and effect lined up. Tissues buried deep within my body relaxed. Electrical currents switched pathways. Rewiring had already begun.

Still, it could take a while for the electricians who manage my gray matter to complete the upgrade. Here's a warning: On occasion you might rush toward me with open arms, face backlit with positive affect. You might smile at me and exclaim, "What a magnificent achievement." (And I certainly hope that comes to pass.) If such a scenario plays out, please don't be alarmed if my eyes glaze over. Or speech slurs. Or my dreadlocks whip around my head like live wires. I'm just short-circuiting.

Watch out for sparks, and back away until the power is restored.

Transcending Tomatoes

MAMA SAID, "THEY'RE good for you."

That mix of slime and seeds and skin? Looked like it oozed from a smashed bug. From that day forward I kept a safe distance from tomatoes.

But when I was fifty, I married a man who adored them fresh from the garden. So, wearing rubber gloves, I sliced them into pretty wedges for my sweetheart.

At fifty-five, I realized my crimson nemesis kicked up the flavor in spaghetti sauce. I hacked them into quarters—for easy identification—and left them behind in the pot when I served myself.

At sixty, I diced them into pea-sized cubes. They snorkeled incognito in my chili. If accidentally spooned up, any offender was gulped down my gullet, bypassing taste buds.

At sixty-four, I ordered vegetarian loaf for lunch. A suspect blood-red glop crowned the dish, but the aromas of thyme, basil, and oregano were mesmerizing; I could no longer see the existential threat in those tomatoes. I scooped up a forkful along with mushrooms and spinach. Acidic tang tangoed with the smoky flavor of portobellos on my tongue. *My God.* Surely the angels serve this dish in Heaven. After six decades, in an instantaneous revelation, I transcended slime, seeds, and skin.

Today, tomatoes. Tomorrow, Everest.

Senior Moment

"YOU'RE SIXTY-FOUR? You'd never know it. You look great."

On hearing this, I grimace. I want to explain why it's not a compliment. I'm on fire to argue against slogans about growing old. Let others strive to be young at heart; let my heart be ageless. Youth is not wasted on the young; nothing is wasted on anyone. Defy my age? No, thanks. This woman's not looking for a fight. Well, maybe she is.

The clichés—as well as my antagonism—miss the mark. In a stampede toward youthfulness, fanatics bypass a quietude that avails itself only to old souls.

What is the word?

Memory fades in and out these days like reception on a cheap TV. Experience teaches me to relax. The word will materialize in a minute or maybe arrive tonight in a dream. My hands hover over the keyboard, the skin wrinkled and translucent. Thick blue veins course from wrist to knuckles. These hands rebut the pseudo-compliments about my appearance. They map a lifetime in ways my unlined face cannot. I hope to use them wisely from now until the end. Stroke my husband's face. Dig holes in the garden for daffodil bulbs. Press into downward facing dog.

Such images cool my resentment and offer a senior's moment of respite. I return to my typing, fingers striking keys, turning tap-tap-tap into prose. Aha. The missing word is *grace*.

Mama's Lament

MONDAY, I WOKE up feeling hopeless. My heart was beating a dirge. I couldn't raise an arm to lift the covers, and even if the action had been possible, I lacked the will to initiate it.

Why? Because it was a Monday? Because dead gray clouds were shrouding the sun? Because Mama had been depressed?

A therapist explained, while I'd slept in utero, chemicals that ferried Mama's malaise through her blood were flowing through mine as well.

A Buddhist teacher said, "It's depression, but not your depression."

Poet Joy Harjo wrote that while she'd listened from an ancestor realm, she'd recognized her mother's song and was called into this world by the music.

On those occasions when Mama, Aunt Gerry, and Aunt Mable replaced their sibling cattiness with harmony, they sounded like the Andrews Sisters. Mama sang alto.

When she called me to be born her daughter, sorrow composed her tune in a minor key.

The pillow that cradled my head offered no comfort. I cupped hands over ears to shut out the songbird melodies floating into the bedroom window, and instead captured the refrain of blood groaning through my veins. Mama's lament.

Center of Attention

AT THE MAPLE Festival, I approached two crafters—drawn to the hand-knitted hats in their booth. "Can you …"

Mary and Nicki were straightening piles of autumn-colored caps.

I fingered a beret. "Could you pick one out for me?"

Nicki said, "Try this one."

Mary plopped a floppy number on my head. She patted and tugged and fluffed, my face the center of her attention.

Her fingertip grazed my temple. I leaned ever so lightly into the spot where skin pressed against skin.

Her hands were kinder than Mama's, which had failed to pat my cheek, failed to braid my hair, failed to articulate my essential prettiness.

"Beautiful," Mary said. She held up a mirror. I peeked. She was right.

For the rest of the day, the maple trees shied away. Their scarlets and oranges dulled in comparison with this blazing cuteness, me in my new hat. The magic chapeau quickened my mood from plod to skip. Perusing other craft booths, I pretended to savor cinnamon-roasted almonds, plucked one at a time from a paper cone—but really, I was enthralled with the soft yarn that caressed my ears, warding off the chill from past neglect.

I snuggled into bed that night, still wrapped in the warmth of my new hat.

The 2015 Dawn-mobile

I'M NOT QUALIFIED to operate this body, having learned to drive in a racier Dawn-mobile. That one went from zero to out-the-door in fifteen minutes. It was sleek. It cornered like nobody's business. The paint job was flawless: no puffy eyes or wrinkled thighs. The engine purred, getting along just fine on the cheapest fuel.

This clunker demands chemical-free, sugar-free 100% whole wheat. Organic quinoa and eggs from pampered chickens. It burns extra virgin olive oil. Dings dimple the bumper. I can ill afford the maintenance: gym memberships, yoga classes, chiropractors, and therapists. And still, it backfires.

As soon as the engine sputtered to life this morning, a headache stabbed at my brow. I downed extra-strength aspirins and left the house for a therapeutic stroll. Caffeine convinced me to speed, but when I pushed the pedal to the metal, this rusty beater only crept up to twenty in the fast lane. The odometer conked out, GPS too, which lengthened the return trip by more miles than my cranky knee appreciated. At the end of the adventure, I put my used-to-be hot rod right back to bed.

For the safety of others who share the highway, authorities ought to require a driver's license for the body I've ended up with. Then again, maybe not. I would definitely fail the vision test.

Too Young for Old Age

I'D GOTTEN TO the age where an elbow, knee, or shoulder either ached or was about to ache. Yet I was told I was too junior to understand anything about being a senior.

Priscilla, who had a few years on me, said, "You're not old enough to know about aging."

I could have argued I was pushing sixty, but I avoided pushing anything that heavy.

I used to be too young to date, then too young to drive, and then too young to vote. Finally, it seemed, I'd grown too young to age.

Caring for a cranky octogenarian provided an opportunity to research this phenomenon. I knew for certain Mr. Cranky was old. He announced it when anything varied his routine.

"You put the cereal in the wrong bowl. I hate this one, and I'm too old to change."

At home, I scoffed at his rigidity as I prepared my own breakfast—oatmeal served up in my special oatmeal bowl. (Its four-inch depth made it far superior to its shallower competitors, which languished, unused.)

Every Monday, Wednesday, and Friday, Mr. C. insisted I fill his favorite bowl with two-thirds cup of Raisin Bran and then add just enough milk to float seven flakes.

Every Monday, Wednesday, and Friday, I pooh-poohed his pickiness. I snorted with disdain as I topped my steaming cereal with four walnuts, seven raisins, two level teaspoons of brown sugar, and one-third cup of warm milk. (Warmed, of course, to prevent it from chilling the cereal.)

Mr. Cranky kept a monthly appointment at the veterans' hospital. On those days he watched the clock with great concern.

"Why isn't my food done yet? You know I have to eat at eight o'clock. Now I'll have to rush to get to the V.A. What's the hold-up?"

The clock read 8:02.

Saturday morning, lost in aggravation over Mr. C's fussiness, I completely forgot about my ten o'clock snack. The clock read 10:17, which meant I would have to rush to keep on schedule for my usual 11:45 lunch break, followed by another snack at three o'clock. My day was ruined.

On the last morning I took care of Mr. C., he was wearing his laundry-day slacks. A narrow belt cinched excess waistband around his skinny frame, gathering in the fullness like a skirt. Pale skin peeked from between the tops of his socks and the hems of his pants.

He greeted me with his customary good cheer. "My shoulder hurts like hell today."

As I drove away from his apartment, I tut-tutted Mr. C.'s transformation from retired bank executive to Red Skelton lookalike. I shook my head as I changed into my favorite Freddy the Freeloader pants. Two sizes too big, they provided just enough extra room to accommodate the brace I'd strapped on underneath. My knee hurt like hell that day.

I hobbled to the kitchen and celebrated my release from Mr. C.'s elderly quirkiness with a bowl of cereal and the latest issue of *AARP The Magazine*.

Priscilla was right. I was too young to know about old.

Migraines, Why Me?

EXTENSIVE ONLINE RESEARCH provided answers: mold, mites, wine, tension, sugar, dust, insomnia, caffeine.

I cultivated snake plants to filter toxins from the air and transformed my diet into organic purity. Laundered the bedding in non-scented detergent, with a bleach chaser. Stripped away carpets—just-waking tootsies slapped against cold wood instead of padding along fleecy wall-to-wall. Out with lilacs fresh from the pollen-infused garden. Away with the sublime poison of chocolate. No more champagne toasts to tickle taste buds. All bases covered, *T*s crossed, and *I*s dotted. My headaches metamorphosed into occasional outliers.

But as I unwound from a yoga contortion, the Godzilla of migraines tore through my body and shrieked its disdain for my sacrifices.

On television, a weather lady mentioned in passing, "... bad time for anyone who suffers from dreaded barometric pressure headaches ..." A storm had blown in overnight; temperatures had plummeted twenty degrees.

My agony caused by ... air? After the Internet provided confirmation, I searched online for cures, but found only eyestrain and despair. What other demons were skulking about, ready to pounce?

The quest for understanding is a pain in the neck. If my head hurts tomorrow, I'll massage these temples with the balm of not-knowing, and pop a couple of aspirins.

Pilgrimage

CHERYL'S HOLIDAY LETTER reported her schedule was "light this year." Five days in Burma, five in Thailand, a week in Virginia, and two five-day reunions.

How did she accumulate such adventures? How did she acquire people with whom to reunite?

The other night, I spent six hours on the couch in front of the television. From the news to a sitcom to a movie to a talk show.

Well, no more of that. It was high time to fill my empty calendar. Well, first thing in the morning.

While I dawdled in bed, in the dreamy space halfway between the night before and the day ahead, a to-do list bloomed. Volunteer to read to pre-schoolers. (I'm serious.) Hike the trail behind the yoga studio. (Not kidding.) Drive to the botanical gardens. (Absolutely committed.) Invite someone to lunch. (It's going on my schedule right now.) Or the art museum. (As good as done.) Or Thailand.

I caught sight of a reflection in the mirror. Me ... looking at me ... looking at me .... rumpled covers kicked aside, yesterday's clothes heaped on the floor, Cheryl's letter folded on the nightstand underneath a glass.

This is my life.

It's rolled out exactly as The Great Intention Behind Everything intended it.

I sit at the computer. I nap. I watch television. If The Great Intention places a pilgrimage to India in my future, it will occur to me to buy a plane ticket.

Speaking of My Life

CALL HER ML for short.

She wasted away the morning zoning out on social media, with detours over to slide shows of the ten worst celebrity plastic surgeries and nine secrets to a transformational pedicure. She then plopped herself onto the couch for some dedicated boob tube study. We're not talking documentaries or BBC. We're talking reality TV. Game shows. Cook-offs. During the commercials, ML daydreamed about upgrading her cell phone to the luxury brand—the one manufactured by exploited Chinese children. At dinnertime, she snarfed up a corn-fed beef burger, on a bun baked with refined white sugar and genetically modified wheat. The fast food place was only three blocks away; you'd think ML would have walked. Lord knows she needed the exercise. But no, she drove her fossil-fuel-burning non-hybrid car.

Between fries, I gave her a good talking to. *Everybody knows you ought to eat organic. You shouldn't spend your money on products that poison the environment. And television ... known fact it will fry your brain. Starting tomorrow, we're making big changes. From now on we're into deep spiritual values.*

As I fussed and worried and planned, ML kicked back to watch *American Idol*.

Problem Solved

A POP-UP AD below the browser's search bar drew my attention away from Dictionary.com. The morning writing routine would have to wait.

Hemingwrite. Clever name. What's that about? A click opened an article describing an invention for writers that was being funded on Kickstarter. A word-processor sans Internet browser, it looked like a flattened-out typewriter with a postcard-sized screen. What a godsend for people like me, easily seduced by online curiosities, tempted to peek at Facebook or open one more email. This might work. Just sit and type while it backs up the document to the cloud, and that's good, because … well let's see how much it costs.

The cursor blinked over the link to the Kickstarter campaign.

A cartoon lightning bolt zapped my head. Eyeballs sproinged from their sockets. A singed dreadlock plopped onto the keyboard.

Here sits a woman absorbed in an Internet article about a device designed to prevent her from reading Internet articles.

Sigh.

Once again stuck on its treadmill, busy mind races toward solutions to problems it creates.

It's not my job to locate a detour from the information highway. My job is to notice I'm distracted and then observe how that feels. Nothing more.

Life works out. It always has. The details are above my pay grade.

How to Give Advice

"YOU AWAKE?" MY husband whispered. Four a.m., our talking time. "Need your help with a problem."

I love giving advice. Love solving problems. Love that he acknowledged my superior intelligence.

"Yeah." Alert. Cheerful. Ready to lay a little wisdom on him.

A conversation with an acquaintance had heated up into disagreement. Ahh. Relationships. My area of expertise. The solution to his problem became clear to me right away. I held my breath. I'd insert my counsel as soon as he paused.

A little voice said *try listening*.

The advice balloon deflated.

Hubby continued, relating his frustration at how the interaction had gone south, and something about feelings, something about fault, until his story petered out.

In the dark, he couldn't see my face scrunched up in an effort to keep quiet. He'd asked for help. Surely he was waiting for my insight. It felt awkward to withhold it. Even rude.

An hour later (okay, maybe ten seconds), he said, "Thanks, Honey. After talking this over with you, I know exactly what to do."

Having said nothing, I was brilliant.

Mother's Day Schematic

A GRAPH PLOTS one woman's emotions over a twenty-four-hour period on the second Sunday in May.

Line 1, bitterness at being wished a happy Mother's Day, rises at the same rate as Line 2, regret at ending up childless. Note that Line 3, despair over the death of her mother, spikes when well-wishers add, "Even if you don't have kids, everybody's got a mom."

Set in My Ways

GOOD MORNING, UNIVERSE. *I'll have the usual.*

Crunchy granola wasn't on the menu. On discovering its absence, I sucked in my breath in disbelief and—let's face it—horror.

I always have crunchy granola for breakfast. (Except, of course, during winter, when I eat creamy, steamy oatmeal.)

Right after showering with my usual body wash and slathering on my usual lotion.

Last week CVS ran out of my deodorant brand, which comes in an easy-to-spot lime green bottle. I was forced to read labels in order to ferret out an alternative that listed the preferred attributes: solid, invisible, unscented. I found it between the high-desert-scented roll-ons and the fragrant-petunia-blossom sprays.

The drugstore hasn't stocked my usual dental tape either. I can't possibly switch to floss. The hygienist said if I don't use the tape, my teeth will fall out.

But who needs teeth when crunchy granola's not on the menu? I'll just gum scrambled eggs.

Nirvana

THE TOWELS WERE shooting off negative energy bolts into our otherwise peaceful home.

My designer bath sheets had lost their dignity, squashed inside the linen closet between a wad of fitted sheets and a sixty-four-pack of toilet paper. They were squeezed onto a shelf too narrow for the job. Whenever I reached for one, they all spilled out, a multi-colored terrycloth heap at my feet.

I dove into that closet, arms windmilling, the *Rocky* theme song pounding in my head. Dun-dun-*duh*. Dun-dun-*duh*. I found an electric toothbrush that had gone missing in 2006. There in the corner—a year's supply of hotel shampoos. My college thesis was stuck between a lemon yellow Egyptian cotton and a faded thrift store reject. I dusted and folded, plumped and patted, until those towels were transformed into nirvana. Color-coded. Right angles. Parallel lines.

My husband's toolbox is shooting off negative energy bolts into our otherwise peaceful home.

Samsara

WHEN AN UPSCALE lifestyle magazine featured a chic pal's Los Angeles home, it turned into a sixteen-page, full-color spread of my jealousy. The green-eyed monster drooled all over her Ming porcelain, then left greasy paw prints on sliding glass doors that framed the city's twinkling nightlights. It hunkered down on her French settee. *What is a settee, anyway?*

I waded knee-deep into envy in order to retrieve my affection.

I emailed quasi-cheery congratulations.

She responded in a nano-second. "Thanks. By the way, I love your blog."

Oh.

My out-of-joint nose melted back into place. The ogre whipped a spray bottle from its hairy pouch and wiped those glass doors clean.

A practitioner of refinement treasured my words. There they were, displayed on her turn-of-the-century Rococo game table, elegantly back-lit. Of course she'd collect them. Of course she would recognize their beauty. Her impeccable taste was well documented.

A Bovine Epiphany

ON A MEDITATION retreat, a dozen women occupied a cabin built in the middle of a grazing pasture. On the first morning, I strolled down a gravel driveway, contemplating the nature of reality. Cows lay snoozing under a shade tree. Lying down? *Don't they sleep standing up?* A loner stood with its ankles in a pond.

Twenty years earlier, I was recruiting rural students for the University of Kansas. High school seniors learned about college. I learned about cow tipping. "Really?" I asked. "How do you tip over a cow?"

"Well, ma'am, they're off balance when they sleep." (Farm kids were very polite.) "So we do it at night." (Also very bright.) "But the owners hate it." (Also mischievous. I liked that.)

As a city girl, I couldn't quite picture how it worked.

On the second morning of retreat, most of the herd had joined the loner at the pond. I kicked at stones while questioning the existence of God. Uh-oh. A rock landed too close to the herd. They turned in my direction. *Do cows bite?*

On the last day, I headed down the drive, pondering the finality of death. A cow lumbered closer. I stopped. He stopped. Lordy, he was bigger than a Volkswagen. And far more sturdy. There was no way in hell you could tip that thing over!

Retreats. Where life's big questions are answered.

A Second Bovine Epiphany

A GRAVEL DRIVE from the cabin to the main road cut through a pasture where a dozen cows grazed. Hiking toward them, I hesitated, leery of anything wearing four legs and a tail. A calf looked up at me, then ambled closer to its mother. (My apologies to the cows for being presumptuous about their relationship.) The little one was cute, until she was obscured by her bigger, meaner mom.

I stopped. My knees quivered.

Mama cow squared herself to the drive, ready to attack. Further ahead, cows were lying close enough to swat me with their tails.

My knees got very fluttery, in addition to the quivering.

Other mooing beasts had closed in from behind. They would definitely breathe on me.

My knees were buckling, in addition to the fluttering and quivering. I prepared to die from bovine cooties.

The monsters got bored and wandered off. And when they left, all the activity in my joints wandered off as well.

I was grateful for such a close-up look at fear. How it rose and fell and passed away. How judgments piled on top of anxiety will spiral you into panic. Maybe I'll take this as a starting point, to accept my whole self once and for all. Yes, from now on, a new mantra: compassion for anxiety.

As we were packing up at the close of our retreat, a woman said, "I saw a bobcat yesterday."

What?

Note to my knees: Are you nuts? You wasted my scaries on cows? There were bobcats out there!

Faith

A GRASSY CARPET sloped toward Greco Roman columns, which guarded the entrance to the Nelson Atkins Museum of Art. Cicadas chirped love songs to potential mates, and cardinals whistled their freedom in the treetops, but I was squeezed between transparent partitions rising high as a stockade. A triangle-shaped labyrinth imprisoned me within glass walls. They formed a corridor that angled off in unexpected directions. Clear as cellophane, the enclosure gave the illusion there were no barriers.

Sunlight bounced off the panes, playing tricks. Was I approaching another woman or a reflection of myself? I confused the way forward with the path behind. Forehead-shaped smudges on the walls announced where some who'd entered earlier had misjudged the design. When I reached out for protection from a similar fate, my palm met glass as cold and hard as flint.

Unease intensified with every step; hunger for the familiar gnawed at my gut. Lungs tightened around breath. My body pulsed in rhythm—crescendos of panic, followed by deliverance when the next turn in the labyrinth revealed itself. Dread marked a turning point; relief marked another.

I began to trust that cadence.

Rewarding my faith, the glass walls guided me to the center and back again, at the end spilling me out onto the lawn.

Ode to Dung Beetles

I'M HAVING A shitty week.

Please don't tell me things will get better. Please don't point out the inherent beauty of my rotten week. Please don't offer to clear my lower chakras of the energy blockage that is obstructing light-filled messages from my guardian angels.

I'm not one to make lemonade from lemons.

Silver linings clash with my complexion.

Rose-colored glasses obscure my view.

Dung beetles serve as my gurus. They eat manure, fight over it, and build nurseries in it. If they lose their way while rolling their prize down the road, they climb aboard to navigate by the stars. While they're up there, number two provides a stage for their happy dance. And they wear BMs as flip-flops to protect their tootsies from the baking savannah. With 8,000 species, you've got to figure these poop pushers know what they're doing. If life continues to pile on like steaming elephant scat, I'll burrow right on in and make myself at home.

Show Pies

AT THE FAIR, hubby and I slouched on a park bench near a livestock barn.

A brushed-and-fluffed cow ambled past, led by a teenaged girl. The steer, tail raised, eased out four perfectly formed mounds onto the sidewalk.

We snickered.

And waited.

A pair of light-up tennies skipped closer, avoiding danger with a twisting leap. Next, a stroller and Birkenstocks maneuvered safely through the hazard by executing a series of hairpin turns. Pink clogs approached.

We leaned forward.

Closer.

We held our breath.

Closer.

Bull's-eye. Maximum squish. Cookie cutter imprint.

"Shit-shit-shit." Pink-clogged teenager screamed. She hopped around one-legged like she'd stepped on hot coals. Smeared the insult into the grass. "Eew."

Her companions howled their derision all the way into the barn.

Those who passed by afterward might have wondered why the middle-aged couple on the bench were clutching their stomachs, with tears streaming down their faces.

Porta-Potty Blues

MY HUSBAND BOOKED us into a cabin for the weekend. He said, "It's got electricity, but no running water. You can shower in the main building."

"Does it have a sink?" I asked.

"No running water."

"Toilet?"

"No running water. We'll take a little porta-potty. Look." He brought in a box from the car and set it on the floor in front of the couch. Out came a miniature Johnny-on-the-spot, a cross between a regular restroom facility and a microwave oven.

I arched an eyebrow.

"Comes with special paper. Biodegradable," he said.

I pooched my lips.

"Worried about privacy? We'll set it up in a corner. I'll turn my back. Or, you can walk to an outhouse in the middle of the night."

I crossed my arms. "I'll fast after lunch." Problem solved. No midnight trek down the trail. No unpleasantness in the cabin.

He peered at me over his glasses. "Longest you ever fasted was an hour."

I uncrossed my arms and unpooched my lips. "Okay. Porta-potty."

City Girl Makes Peace with Nature:

Lesson One

NATURE EQUALS TREES, i.e. ticks dropping out of them, spider webs stretched between them, and snakes coiled at their roots. I walk for exercise every day, but choose treadmills—a preference born from an aversion to leafy hiding places.

Easter morning, my husband and I hiked in Missouri's Wallace State Park. He studied the map painted on a wooden placard and selected Rocky Ford Trail. A chilly breeze brushed my face as we crossed a meadow and headed for the trail. After taking a couple of steps straight ahead, I noticed Ben had headed off to the right. He didn't seem to notice my absence.

I closed the gap between us. "How the hell did you know to turn?"

He pointed to a spot a couple yards beyond where he'd stopped. Sure enough, there was a trail, but it petered out into the patch of weeds at my feet. My attempt to understand the natural world was doomed. Mother Nature had failed to provide me the gene that signals where to change direction in the absence of street signs.

Clearly marked from that point, the trail paralleled a stream and cut through oaks still naked from winter. Bone white sycamore skeletons reached skyward. Away from the meadow, the air had stilled. Chill gave way to the sun's heat. We stopped to admire a waterfall trickling over a limestone shelf. Cardinals sang accompaniment to the gurgling creek. I held my breath to take in the music, which nourished even a room-service kind of girl like me.

Today's lesson: Listen.

Multi-Lingual Flu

SICK AGAIN. MY body aches too much to do any doing. I can't sleep for all the helpmates crowded into my bed, who proffer advice while they yank the blankets off my feet.

A babushka'd grandmother, smelling of Vicks, wails at the ceiling in the language of Disaster. This will turn into pneumonia and you'll miss your workouts and gain fifty pounds and have to buy bigger clothes and go broke from the expense. Who will love you then?

I reach for a cough drop, but a Holistic Healer plucks it from my hand. She tut-tuts in dulcet Chakra tones. You might as well eat candy. Your flu always begins with a scratchy throat, doesn't it? She nods, confirming the obvious. Fifth chakra. You have trouble speaking your truth.

I roll away from her condescension, only to end up nose-to-nose with an amateur therapist. She scolds me in clipped Psychobabble. Typical case. You create dis-ease in your body. Avoid success by hiding in your bedroom. She snatches away my pillow.

A nagging mother, fluent in Guilt, pokes me between the shoulder blades. You know better than this. You should have taken at least ten thousand milligrams of vitamin C. Get out of the house more often to toughen up your immune system. I'm disappointed in you. Wait till your father gets home, young lady.

I stumble out of bed to find my husband, who's on the couch watching a football game. As runny nose competes with coughing fits, I crumple onto his shoulder in a soggy heap.

He pats my head. "Sorry you feel bad, Honey. It'll be okay."

He speaks Sweetheart.

The Ties that Bind

The Ties that Bind

"WELCOME TO VICTORIOUS Life Church. Will you fill out a visitor's card?" The woman's voice was a strained whisper.

"Well, sure." I searched through my bag. "If you find my glasses for me."

She laughed, hoarse, and offered me her own specs.

Her rasp triggered my maternal instincts. "Should you be at home in bed?"

"No. It's a disc problem. C5 to C7 got injured. It affects my voice."

"Omigosh. Were you in an accident? Do you still hurt?"

Years earlier, when another driver had plowed his car into mine, ambulance drivers had rattled off similar numbers as they'd strapped me to a backboard. I accumulated four more accidents after that one. I was young and only shaken up each time, never bothered seeing a doctor. But in my fifties, a chiropractor attributed an on-again-off-again ache in my neck to chronic whiplash.

Ms. Victorious Life said, "Yeah. An accident. I hurt all the time."

Brakes screeching, metal slamming against metal, glass shattering. In a flash, an ordinary day is transformed into a procession of hospitals, prescriptions, and pain.

I handed her the completed card, along with her glasses.

"They were going to operate," she said. "But there was a risk of ending up a paraplegic." She placed the card on a stack.

"I decided against surgery." The glasses slipped into her pocket. "Easier to handle whispering to people."

I wanted to hold our conversation close, hoped it would remind me to be kind to the next soul who crossed my path. I wanted to remember the ties that bind us.

The Day I Turned White

MY BROTHER MICHAEL was reciting family history. "… and Mama's mother was white."

What—?

My cousins, siblings, and I were squeezed into Uncle Al's condo for his eighty-fifth birthday. Aunt Ruth, recording our family reunion with her camera, probably caught me open-mouthed.

White—?

Judging from the overwhelming non-reaction in the room, the information was common knowledge. Conversation continued as though Michael had said Mama's mother was *short*. My maternal grandmother had died before I was born. No photos survived. If grandma had been white, what was I?

Will a congressional subcommittee take back all those Affirmative Action prizes, like my college education? Do I forfeit the title of First Black Girl at Santa Barbara High School to Wear an Afro? Inform Ben our marriage is no longer interracial? Need I rescind my edginess at being the sole African American in book group, yoga class, grocery line, craft fair, gallery opening, retreat center, hiking trail, IKEA store?

Embarrassed by ignorance of my own ethnicity, I cornered Michael in the kitchen, where no one else could hear. "Mama's mother. You said she was white?"

"No," he said. "Mama's *grand*mother was white."

Oh.
Never mind. Still black. Keeping the swag.

Post Office Paradox

THE LINE AT the post office inched forward whenever one of the two clerks muttered, "Help-you." Both women glared at us over their reading glasses, which made the phrase more an accusation than an offer. Between mumbles, they shouted. "Need some relief out here." "She still ain't back from lunch?" It was unclear to whom their entreaties were directed, perhaps an Oz-like wizard behind the back wall.

At another branch, I queued up with three other customers. Our instructions were scribbled on a sign beside the clerk. "Be courteous! Don't approach Counter until I say." After handing change to a gentleman, she looked at the ceiling, her hands raised in exasperation. "What are all these people doing in my lobby?"

The Post Office Paradox is Uncle Al. On the one hand, he's a USPS retiree. On the other, it's well documented he's the most-loved man on planet Earth. If you asked him for a stamp, Uncle Al would give you his last one, make you popcorn, sit you in his recliner with your favorite DVD (he'd know which one), and drive your letter to the addressee.

Yesterday, I trudged into yet another branch, schlepping my postal worker prejudice. I stopped short. Then smiled at the clerk. That employee in the blue uniform was somebody's Uncle Al.

Michelle's Face

MY FACE DISAPPEARED.

In the bathroom mirror, it was wrinkled.

In the closet mirror, my features were smooth.

In the make-up mirror, dark circles begged for an additional hour's sleep.

In the rear-view mirror, bright eyes prodded me to conquer the world.

Which countenance was mine?

The day I Skyped my sister, Michelle, her face filled my computer screen. It was beautiful. The expressions that skipped across it were familiar. Our hairlines matched. Our noses, too. When she laughed, I saw my teeth. (She laughed a lot that day, and so did I.)

There's my face. Michelle's been wearing it.

Sunday Morning

AT CHURCH, A spotless kindergarten boy sat between a silver-haired man and woman. The couple, he in a three-piece suit, she in a floral dress with matching broad-brimmed hat, was as rigid as a pair of soldiers at attention. Chomping on a piece of gum, the little one inspected the ceiling, his shoes, and the underside of the gentleman's necktie. He removed the gum and examined it. Madame withdrew a tissue from her purse. She held it in front of the wiggler. Without a word between them, he deposited the glob. She stopped singing just long enough to lean over and kiss her boy on the top of his head.

I beheld this miracle and praised God.

Baby Powder

IN MY TWENTIES, I was paid to adore babies. Freshly fed and diapered, little ones looked up at me as I crossed the threshold into my office—a daycare center. Those who'd mastered the skill crawled over to babble hello. I lowered myself to the floor, patted chubby cheeks, and imagined infants of my own. Stroked downy hair as wispy as my longing. Would I settle for two children? Or a houseful? A strawberry blonde climbed up my shirtfront to stand on wobbly legs. She tasted my top button, her hiccup-giggle scented with applesauce. One day, my cherubs would stamp their feet like she does.

Forty-something. I clacked into the break room on high heels, past a clutch of female colleagues clucking around a pregnant secretary. An office mate said, "Once the nurse lays her on your chest, you'll forget everything else." The pronouncement stung. It exposed my ignorance of broken water and labor pains. It threatened to shake loose the unspoken word *regret*. Motherhood at first postponed, then abandoned. Other roads were taken.

Sixty-something. In line behind a young mother, whose red-haired baby waved from his seat in the grocery cart. His contagious gurgle pulled me toward him, but not quite close enough to pat his dimpled knee. He raised his pudgy fist to his nose, then pulled it away for a round of peek-a-boo. Mom snapped her purse shut and pushed the cart toward the doors, her carrot-topped boy singing, "Ma ma ma ..." Bittersweet scent of baby powder in his wake.

Little Lambs Choir

THE CHOIR DIRECTOR prompted them as they faced the congregation. "Get all excited. Tell all about it. Jesus Christ is born." She held a hand mike in front of each little face in turn.

A star in red velvet squealed. She flipped her beaded braids like Marilyn Monroe. "Get all—"

A chubby-cheeked boy behind her grabbed the mike. "—excited. Tell all—"

A slender soloist in a three-piece suit leaned back and belted, his mouth an O wide enough to fit a double cheeseburger. "—about it. Jesus—"

The entire group shouted the last line together. (Except for a beauty in a pink leather skirt who missed her cue. Hands on hips, she was striking runway poses.) They disagreed on the tune. "—Christ is born."

I shook with laughter. And grieved my own lost innocence.

Christmas Adopt-a-Family

I SLOGGED INTO the Salvation Army offices to volunteer, wishing I were home in front of the television. It had seemed like such a good idea when I'd said yes to a friend who'd asked for help on behalf of her church group. Christmas spirit and all that. In the gym I plucked a form from a stack on the volunteer registration table. The paper listed members of an anonymous family: first names, ages, gift requests. I joined my teammate beside a plastic trash bag bursting at the seams with packages. Our job was to match the contents against the items on the form. At least thirteen million bags were scattered across the gym, all overflowing. I would never see home again.

My teammate plucked a fashion doll from our first sack. The form read "Kimmy, age seven, Barbie." Check.

Next, a football. "Reginald, ten, sports." Check.

A pair of Iron Man pajamas. "Andy, eight, superheroes." Check.

A lump rose in my throat. I was holding an honest-to-goodness Christmas List.

One pair of Uggs. "Marnie, six, fuzzy boots." They were a nine on the Richter scale of cuteness. When I checked them off the list, my hand shook.

The children's mother had penciled a note across the bottom of the form. "… working two jobs … husband just laid off. Hope we won't need this help again, but we're grateful …"

Next year? I'll be back.

Wearing an elf hat.

Best Friends

WE HADN'T SPOKEN for months when she called. "You get the alumni magazine?"

I felt guilty because I hadn't phoned her first. "Yeah. Right here."

"Page sixty-one," she said. "Jeannette died."

"Who?"

"You're kidding." She sounded annoyed.

I tried to remember, wanted to share girlfriend gossip.

"Our freshman dance teacher," she said

"Sure. Jeannette."

"You don't know who she is, do you? Didn't college mean anything to you?"

I searched for an answer, but found only blurred images, faint voices.

She said, "Well . . . I've got to run. Bye."

"How's your mom?"

"Still a pain. See you . . . sometime. Bye."

"Bye."

Our last words stung long after I snapped my phone shut.

From Dawn to Daylight

A Principled Woman

MS. AFRICAN AMERICAN Icon looks skinnier on her magazine cover than she did on television last week. She's lost at least forty pounds on a Photoshop diet.

No, no. Not her at all ... that face is three shades lighter than hers. But who is it? Wait a minute. Might be her. Has she lightened her skin? Impossible. Never. Damn.

She *has* lightened her skin.

Where's my Girlfriend, who faced her body image struggles out loud and in public? You inspired me to work through mine. I cheered when you hauled out your wagonload of fat. And commiserated two sizes later, after you fell off the wagon. I followed you from fad diets to personal trainer. My Black Woman Who Made Good. Black, as in eighty percent cacao, not white chocolate. What about me?

Give back my loyalty, Ms. Icon. Your magazine cover's a bait and switch. It screams you prefer a slender, light-complexioned body to the reality. It screams you've bought into the phony ideal of beauty you've been preaching against. What lies did you tell yourself to justify this trampling of your principles?

Then again, what lies do I tell ... to justify my trampling of your character? In a single rant, I shaved away forty pounds of empathy and at least three shades of heart.

Love Letter to Donald Sterling

DEAR DONALD,

I'm as shocked to be writing this as you must be to read it.

The first three times your face flashed across my television screen, I did not understand all the hullabaloo. Big deal. An NBA owner said something racist. And the players? They knew your values every time they cashed their paychecks. So, please, a bunch of rich men squabbling among themselves. Where's the news?

Avoiding a commercial on another network, my channel-surfing husband landed on your CNN interview. "Look at that face. Really, you've got to feel sorry for him." (And here's a good reason to avoid marriage: Your spouse will annihilate your superiority complex with a kind remark right out of the blue.)

Against my will, I breathed in my husband's words. You did not arrive into this moment a full-blown media villain. Life placed you on earth as an innocent baby boy, whose mother probably said, "Look at that face."

Sigh.

Life composed your words, which I labeled racist, as surely as Life wrote, "I have a dream." Life gave you wealth, as surely as It made Siddhartha a prince. It expressed Itself through your confusion, as surely as It radiated through Christ's compassion.

And so, against my will, against all logic, Donald Sterling, my teacher, I love you.

Yours truly,

From Dawn to Daylight

Chicagoland

A DOCUMENTARY FOLLOWED the challenges of an urban high school principal, desperate to keep her students alive and out of jail. Despite her efforts, a favored young man—call him Tony—landed behind bars. She visited him weekly, tutored him through his GED, lobbied successfully for his early release.

When the prison gate closed behind him and he spotted her in the parking lot, he ran to her—a child again, wrapped in a mother's embrace. His face was lit with affection, innocence, and optimism. He'd made it.

The documentary followed his progress after his release. The principal located a halfway house and helped him move in. A mentor arranged for a job interview. He made plans to drive Tony to the meeting. My excitement mounted. An urban cliché was being transformed into happily ever after. But Tony neglected to set his alarm clock. He missed the interview and then disappeared. His story line picked up again with him back in jail, charged with robbery.

Why? I needed to blame someone. And the logical choice was Tony. He wasted all those opportunities to transform his life. Why couldn't he manage to set an alarm clock?

Eastern mystic Ramesh Balsekar said humans act according to their nature. I am created with a set of characteristics. Life expresses through me according to those characteristics. If life were to have expressed through Tony as a boy who made his way out of the ghetto, he would have thought, *I need to set my alarm.* Instead, life expressed as a Tony who would spend more time in jail.

I live in my own Chicagoland, stuck in situations I should have powered through by force of self-discipline, blaming myself for failure to transform.

But no ... there's no one to blame. Tony and I are innocent.

Betrayed

I STARTLED AWAKE this morning, blind-sided twenty years after the fact.

My first husband's best friend touched my crotch. We were giving him a tour of our new house. I'd paused in the dining room. As the buddy followed my husband past me into the living room, the back of his hand grazed my skirt. Right There. His knuckles tapped, subtle, a move only an experienced groper could have pulled off.

Simultaneous reactions screamed *he did not do that* and *holy crap, he did.* Contact in that vicinity, even the lightest pat, does not go unnoticed. Sensation-wise, sirens blared and horns blasted. Neon arrows and helicopter searchlights pointed directly to The Spot.

My mind doubted, but my body knew.

I ignored my body. I built a wall of protection, retreated into stoic muteness, while the two men chatted about gospel music.

They were colleagues, the friend a successful manager trailing a string of whispered allegations from promotion to promotion. He reported to my husband, who'd heard the workplace rumors, but believed his friend. Why not? None of the women could prove a thing.

Neither could I.

I kept the story to myself, on the day it happened and on every other day during our marriage.

I startled awake this morning, blind-sided twenty years after the fact. Failing to trust him, I had betrayed my first husband.

Invisible Man

MY BROTHER'S PLANE was late. I passed the time by pacing, exchanging hellos as I navigated through the mob. I expected Wayne to roll through the gate in his chair. When it came to expanses as long as airport concourses, he usually wheeled. Around the house, he walked. But he showed up at the gate on foot, backpack and coat piled on his wheelchair.

"Hey, Wayne, that looks pretty funny, you pushing your backpack."

"Tired of sitting on that damn plane. I need to walk."

I tried to imagine a six-footer like him folded into those seats.

"Well, hell, I'll ride in the chair and you can push me."

I plopped myself down and set the backpack in my lap, twisting around in the seat to gossip while we made our way to baggage claim. When we arrived at the carousel, he parked me and then waded into the mob to wrangle his duffel bag.

A man popped out of the crowd, heading toward me. I opened my mouth to say hello. At the last second he averted his gaze and hurried past. A woman approached. I smiled up at her. "Hi," I said. She seemed to locate my voice. Her head bent in my direction, but just as our gazes were about to intersect, she turned away. One after another, they glanced away, their gazes bouncing off the top of my head like basketballs hitting the rim.

"The weirdest thing happened," I said to Wayne. "I've become invisible."

"Yeah. Welcome to my world."

Basketball Moves

I ADMIRE HOW basketball players fall. Splat on the belly and then slide across the floor, slick as a sled down a snowy hill. Or they thud onto the butt and pop up as though it were part of a tumbling run. They leap right back into the game.

The winter I lost my footing on an icy sidewalk, my hand took the brunt of it; the upshot was a broken wrist that put me out of the game for months. It was an artless tumble. Strictly amateur.

My husband and I checked into the Y for our usual cardio. When we turned the corner from the welcome desk, athletes in wheelchairs swirled around us and spilled out from the gymnasium doors. Guys and girls, men and women, from peewee league to NBA hopefuls, they were in town for a regional basketball tournament.

We climbed into the bleachers, along with other fans. As in all endeavors, a star emerged, the kid with genius moves. He was fast, graceful, smart, and accurate. Both legs were missing from the hip down, his right arm amputated at the elbow. A seat belt strapped him into the chair. As he executed a series of intricate fakes, dribbling into position for a three-pointer, his chair rolled over. It pinned him underneath, wheels in the air, spinning. I couldn't tell how it got worked out—I'm often six moves behind while watching a game—but he was upright and sinking a free throw before I could gasp. Before my respect finished its artless freefall into pity.

I admire how basketball players fall.

My New Office

"HONEY, I WANT an office. Where I can close the door and write."

My husband chuckled. "The whole house is your office."

True. The patio. The couch. The kitchen—laptop on the counter, so I can stand while typing. In fact, closed doors make me claustrophobic.

Dee and I were admiring her garden. I said, "Writing at home is wonderful, but Ben likes to tell me about the news. Hard to say *don't talk to me*." We strolled past a bird feeder. "If I had a signal ... maybe stick something in my hair."

"I've got it!" She led me into her family room where she rummaged through a cabinet until she found a box filled with cat toys and pulled out an orange plastic feather. "Ta dah."

Sticking it in my ponytail, I checked myself in a mirror. "Yeah. This could work."

Ben agreed to try it. Still, I was nervous about upsetting our routine.

After sunrise, I plodded into the spare bedroom, stuck the feather in my hair, and picked up the laptop. I settled into a wing-back chair, the door to the hallway open beside me. Downstairs, the blender whirred. Floorboards creaked. The energy in the house vibrated, telegraphing that Ben had already perused CNN.com.

"Those damn—" A foot crossed the threshold. He screeched to a halt. I typed. Silence. I typed faster. He tiptoed down the hallway. Yeah. This could work.

From Dawn to Daylight

Remembering Stef

CAN IT BE a year since Stef died? Wasn't it yesterday I'd fallen in love with her?

Before illness took over, she'd emailed me, troubled. An acquaintance of hers had accused her of making a comment that was racially charged.

Back then, I was mistaking spirituality for a carte blanche to analyze my loved ones. I replied, "Maybe you're upset because you really are prejudiced, and you don't want to face it." I threw in some Buddhist jargon for good measure.

A week later, her email response. "I'm furious with you. I've been pacing around my house trying to figure out what to do about it. I didn't ask you to teach me something. I wanted you to listen."

Her words shriveled my hubris. I recognized myself—that damned impulse to spout my opinions about your real motivation, as I saw it.

"Can we meet for coffee, to talk this through?" she asked.

I was grateful for the chance to apologize in person. "Yes!"

We crowded our coffee, pastries, and roiling emotions onto a tiny wrought iron table.

She said, "I couldn't let this go, but the idea of hashing it out face to face ... well, it scared me. What if you got mad ... ended our friendship? Then I realized that would have to be okay. I want relationships where I can be honest."

"Me too, Stef. I'm really sorry."

We talked it through. (I listened.)

I miss that Stef, willing to reach for my hand, willing to slog through the muck side by side.

Goodbye, Roger Ebert

NEWS ACCOUNTS REPORTED you died after a long battle with cancer.

After having inspired millions, having fallen hopelessly in love with a powerful woman who loved you back . . . falling for each other again every day for twenty years, having played at your chosen profession as long and as hard as you chose, having declared, "I am as I should be," and having earned a Pulitzer Prize to boot.

Note to my survivors: If my life looks anything like Ebert's (and thank you, Lord, if it does, sans Pulitzer and the inspiring of millions), when I die, do not say I fought a battle.

A Pope for Thich Nhat Hanh

EVEN THOUGH I'M not Catholic, I was watching television, waiting for white smoke to billow from the Sistine Chapel's chimney.

As Pope Francis stepped onto the balcony, there was a catch in my throat, even though …

He smiled easily. He joked. His voice soft and small against the storms awaiting him. One old man, shouldering the hopes of a billion people. When he asked us to pray for him, I closed my eyes along with the faithful crowded into St. Peter's Square, even though …

Thich Nhat Hanh said, "Call me by my true names."

For now, before my opinions reclaim my attention, call me catholic.

Pope Francis: The Latest Next Big Thing

THE PUBLIC HAS become enamored with our first non-European pontiff. The day after he was elected pope, he returned to the boardinghouse—where he'd stayed in the lead-up to the conclave—to pay his bill. He washed the feet of prisoners. He kissed the face of a disfigured man. He snuck away from the Vatican to walk the streets of Rome, giving alms to the poor. *The New York Times* reported he telephoned a divorced Italian woman—pregnant by a married man—to offer her comfort. He eschewed lavish apartments in the Apostolic Palace, to take up residence in the Vatican guesthouse. Why, he even blessed a rally of 35,000 leather-clad bikers in St. Peter's Square.

What ever happened to that other His Holiness who warmed our secular hearts? The one who said, "Be kind whenever possible. It is always possible."

Mr. Dalai Lama, Mr. Manifestation of the Bodhisattva of Compassion … inspiration-wise, what have you done for me lately?

Rare Birds

DEAR LITTLE JUNCO,

You were the first rare bird to find our feeder. The sparrows that preceded you were nothing to marvel at. I felt quite important when my friend Sarah pointed you out, way back under the evergreen.

"See that little black bird out there?" she said.

And I did. My first day of bird watching, and already I excelled.

"So cute," Sarah said.

"He is," I replied.

"He'll poke around right here under the feeder, if he approves your seed."

That was last week, Little Junco. Every day since, you and a couple dozen of your buddies have been hopping around among those un-marvelous sparrows. Under the feeder, and on the feeder, too, where frankly, Sarah says you're not supposed to go. So, Little Junco, please do me a favor. Take your gang to somebody else's backyard. I need the space for that darling black-capped chickadee that's waiting over there in the redbud tree. Just look at that chubby thing—like a tennis ball with a beak. Isn't he irresistible?

Sincerely,
The Management

City Girl Makes Peace with Nature:

Lesson Two

ON THE WAY to the mailbox, I leaned over to pull out dandelions popping up through the cracks in the driveway. I grabbed sturdy leaves in a bunch, my knuckles scraping concrete, and I yanked. Another plant seemed to pop up every time I plucked. They were cartoon dandelions; each taproot connected to the top of another dandelion in the ground beneath it, whose taproot was connected to the next, an endless chain all the way down to China. *That's it. Time for reinforcements.*

Bring on fungicides, pesticides, herbicides, and any other cides on the market.

The idea shriveled up, dead on the vine. A sensation I'd never felt before crept across my sweaty palm, informing me I would not be using any weed killer. It stopped my bomb-'em-back-to-the-Stone-Age plans as effortlessly as a red light stops my car.

I quit using chemicals in the yard a couple years ago, because of the environmental impact on ground water and pollinators. Blah blah blah. This new feeling didn't give a hoot about all those fancy words. It was unimpressed by my intellectual prowess and unconcerned with ecological issues. It simply zapped away the distance between Dawn the Gardener and Betty the Bee.

I'll pull weeds by hand. Spraying poison would be shooting myself in the foot.

Today's lesson: disarm.

Racist Recipe

A CELEBRITY CHEF, renowned for Southern cuisine, was overheard mixing racial slurs into her conversation, as deftly as she sprinkled salt into her fried chicken batter. Shortly after that revelation, a video surfaced that showed her restaurant servers costumed as slaves. Her shocked publisher pulled the contract for her upcoming cookbook. A television network threatened to cancel her show. Social media erupted.

Her champions—or apologists, depending on your viewpoint—leapt to her defense. "It's cultural . . . Southern women her age say nigger from time to time . . . who doesn't?"

"Cultural? I'm going to scream." Irene, my (white) online writing partner, said.

I was astounded that a white acquaintance was voicing my own outrage.

Irene's outburst interrupted our email exchange about whether the last sentence in her manuscript called for a semicolon or a period. When we weren't dissecting grammar, Irene and I exchanged marketing leads and pricing tips. I didn't know she *could* scream.

Turns out, her roots ran deep through Southern states. Her grandmother from rural Alabama lived till ninety-six and " . . . tolerated no one who said that word within her hearing."

"I like your grandmother," I replied.

"Not talking . . . is the problem," she said.

What a marvel that she wanted to talk about a subject personal to me. And how miraculous she was the one who'd brought it up. She didn't have to care about race, yet she did. Enfolded into her protective outrage, I felt as cherished as a child.

Irene and I had been merely colleagues, until that celebrity cook's pinch of racism turned us into friends.

Seven Regrets

1. Losing Anthony.
2. Failing to attend my brother's college graduation.
3. Skipping an awards dinner for my father, who died three months later.
4. Switching my undergrad major from Spanish to American Studies.
5. Passing up the chance to study abroad when I was a sophomore.
6. Not having children.
7. Forgetting the name of the sweet girl my parents took in, who was preoperational from boy to girl.

How Far Do You Need to Walk?

BEN AND I pace around the indoor track at the YMCA. There are days when he prods me to go. Others when I prod him. The track leads us in circles—boring, but it's good for us. One mile for health.

A mother in East St. Louis locks her kids in the apartment and plods past a liquor store on the corner, a McDonald's beyond it, and a payday loan down the block. She heads for the supermarket nearest her redlined neighborhood, to buy what she can carry. Five miles for food.

A man, woman, and boy flag down a car. The woman asks the driver, "Will you take us to Wal-Mart?"

He answers, "There's none around here."

She says, "It's by the HyVee across town."

After they climb in, the driver's wife asks, "Walking? Where do you live?"

"City Union Mission. We don't have a car. My sandals broke again and Walmart's always cheapest." Twelve miles for shoes.

Siblings in Sudan flee from soldiers who killed their parents, burned their village, and kidnapped their brother. The second-oldest boy, now their chief, leads them across a desert. They drink urine and hide from lions, before stumbling into a Kenyan refugee camp. A thousand miles for safety.

I poke my head into Ben's office. "I'm going to bed. You?" He's staring at the computer screen.

"Be there in a while."

"Okay, nighty-night." I lean over in my jammies, to offer a kiss. He grins at me and closes his laptop.

"Changed my mind. I'm coming now." Zero miles for love.

Closure

Interrupted Conversation

MAY. OH MY. An actual email hidden between the LinkedIn message and the so-and-so-liked-your-Facebook-post. Chris, a long-missing friend, had updated her address.

"What's new?" I asked.

"Glioblastoma multiforme."

A Google search filled in details. I calculated a six-month prognosis.

June. I asked, "When you think about dying, are you afraid?"

"I don't know," she said. "Because what comes next ... is nothing."

July. She said, "I don't have enough lounge wear."

My siblings visited that summer. Evenings we changed into sweats to hang out after dinner. Michelle swept down the stairs in a Loretta Young gown, her entrance all bosomy and fabulous. We applauded.

August. I said, "I'm jealous of my sister's pretty lounge wear."

Chris said, "You be pretty. I'll take comfort."

Our conversation lagged, her email buried ever deeper in my inbox, beneath coupons, yoga studio updates, and water bills.

October. "Now where were we?" I asked.

She didn't answer.

Seven Fragrances I Miss

1. Dad's pipe tobacco. He couldn't criticize while he puffed.

2. Ivory soap. The bar that floated. After my bath, I was 99.44% pure. My impurities left a ring around the tub.

3. Pine-Sol. Mother cared enough about me to mop the floor I walked on.

4. Chalk dust. It collected in the tray beneath the blackboard in high school Spanish class and sifted into the air as I passed notes to the football star two seats over.

5. Newsprint ink. I proofed the copy for want ads, ferreted out typos from freshly printed pages. A solitary summer job in the basement of the News-Press, my hermit sanctuary.

6. Shalimar. A dab on my throat. I bought it often when I was single. A gift from me to me.

7. Eucalyptus trees. At the Vedanta Society in Santa Barbara. My husband, brother, sister, and I meditated at vespers. Eucalyptus blessed our prayers.

Old Photos

I DRAGGED A dust-covered box of photos from my closet. It was headed straight for the trash. Once it was gone I'd be able to pluck a dress from its hanger without stubbing my toe on the carton. My mantra for the day: declutter.

A final push would have propelled that box through my bedroom door and into the hallway, but it occurred to me I might salvage picture frames for Goodwill.

I lifted the lid. A high school portrait lay on top of the stack, my expression falsely serene. I was the new girl at school. Girl cliques spat insults at me. Boys hurled lewd come-ons.

And here, my siblings, Michael and Michelle, just five years old. Because they're twins, they were posed like bookends. They sat on the floor back-to-back, arms hugged around their knees, a row of hymnals stretched between them. Was that the year Dad threw Michael onto the sidewalk, because he was afraid to go fight a bully?

And this—a family Christmas shot. Back in the 1970s, when I wore my hair in an Afro and my skirts barely covered my underwear. My face bore the expression of an inmate facing hard time. I didn't celebrate holidays back then; I was condemned to them.

Weighted with pain, the photos proved too heavy for me to lug to the trash. I shoved the coffin of memories back into my closet.

Two years later, I dragged it out again. Who was that young woman with the calm expression? Whose children, mugging for the camera? Who are those people surrounded by holiday trimmings? Faces whose stories I could no longer recall.

Forgive Me

I HAVE TO apologize.

Again.

I'd expressed an appropriate level of remorse fifteen years ago. She still refused to talk to me.

Her absence left a gaping hole.

For over a decade, I conjured her image during metta practice, when meditation teachers instructed, "Send loving kindness to a difficult person."

Retreats, dharma talks, and voyages through bleak internal landscapes eventually revealed an unwelcome truth: The difficult person was me. Fifteen years ago, my apology had meant *Sorry you're inflexible. Sorry you're mad. Sorry you don't understand my position.*

Today, it means *I put myself inside your life and come up as angry with me as you were.*

I'm going to apologize again.

And then forgive myself.

Seven Wonders of the World

1. The bundle of brush my husband gathered to set out on the curb.
2. Dandelions. I plucked one whose taproot was at least two feet long.
3. Our spotless kitchen counter, a surprise accompaniment to this morning's breakfast.
4. The driver who waved me across the street while I was walking.
5. A freshly scrubbed toilet. Any time. Anywhere.
6. The leaf that unfurled yesterday on the dieffenbachia, shiny as a new dime.
7. Shiny dimes. Where will they travel? They gleam with possibility.

Chocolate Cake

I'VE VISITED FRIENDS in four hospitals in the space of a single month. Heart attack here, cancer there, pneumonia in between. Illness has swooped down from the tundra on a misery-laden jet stream. Now my husband's sick—a hacking cough, his thanks for taking care of me last week when I was down with the flu. That's life. I shouldn't be surprised.

Doug brought us a chocolate cake he'd baked from scratch, his specialty. After he left us to our tissues and aspirin, I set the treat between Ben and me on the couch, like a hookah. We waved the scent of cocoa into our beleaguered sinuses, then raised our forks, as we grunted in thanksgiving for this unexpected gift from heaven.

Unexpected?

That 's life. I shouldn't have been surprised.

Monsoon

THROUGH THE RAIN pelting my windshield, I could make out only a string of blinking brake lights. I'd snapped off the radio thinking I'd see better without it, and anyway, the downpour that sledge-hammered the roof had drowned out the newscaster's soothing monotone. An SUV in the next lane was about to crush me from the right side, and you could have surfed on the wave thrown up by a cocky four-by-four as it sped in the opposite direction down Southwest Trafficway. Shoulders hunched in concentration, jaw clenched, I white-knuckled the steering wheel. Lightning arced over the line of traffic, followed too soon by a thunderclap explosion that caused a spastic hop in my left leg. "Shit. I'm going to die out—."

Before the sentiment could reach its terror-drenched conclusion, it was washed away by its own essential truth, as though my human essence could hold either the fear of my demise, or its certainty—not both at once.

Annihilation had always been right here at my shoulder, rather than a dozen car lengths ahead, where brake lights disappeared into the storm. Death in fact had copiloted this vessel from the start.

My grip on the steering wheel eased. I opened the window a crack to catch the scent of rain.

It was a good day to die. I was in love. The house was clean.

Radiation Therapy Waiting Room

A MIDDLE-AGED WOMAN trudged into the waiting room alone, while I waited for a friend. The new patient signed in and then slumped into a chair beside me. Was she staring at my dreadlocks?

"Hi. How're you doing?" I asked.

"I did *not* have a good weekend." Her gaze fixed on my face longer than comfort usually allows between strangers. "Started to lose my hair."

"I'm so sorry."

"I used to have a head full," she said.

"Is it coming out in clumps?"

"By the handfuls." She made a fist. "I don't want to wear a wig." She pounded her knee, then turned away, waiting.

Corpse Pose

WHERE WILL YOU die?

A fan of irony, I plan to die in the living room.

I'll first set a folder—containing my will and a list of passwords—on the coffee table. Beside the documents, the Kindle will be powered up, cycling through MP3s of Tibetan monks accompanied by singing bowls. I'll unfurl my yoga mat onto the freshly dust-mopped hardwood floor, perform a final round of sun salutation, and lie in savasana, dreadlocks spread like sun rays around my face. Monastic choirs will ohm me into eternity.

A fantasy death to end a fantasy life.

Candlelight Vigil

ON A FRIGID December night, my husband and I pulled into the parking lot of St. James Catholic Church to join a candlelight vigil against gun violence. Parishioners were already gathered on the corner, their candle flames a minor constellation within a universe of traffic lights. I pulled two tapers from my purse, as our friend Kate—a church member, she'd invited us—parked her car near ours. We paraded toward the group, and, claiming spots against a wall, blended into the background.

The national news had been filled with stories about unarmed black boys and men killed by police officers, while the local news had been decrying the frequency of homicides in city neighborhoods.

I set aside my opinions about race relations in twenty-first century USA. On 39th and Troost in midtown Kansas City, I held a candle. We were only a few, our presence on that sidewalk brief, but I felt consoled with my hands folded in prayer around a taper. Drivers tapped their horns; some waved, and the gestures brought us together in sorrow and united us in our exhaustion from grieving. A gust sneaked up my coat sleeve. I shivered. It was a night to mourn.

No Longer Mother

CANCER SHRANK MOTHER'S sweater-girl figure until she was a speck in her hospital bed, which had replaced her California king. Her sketchpad topped a stack of books on the floor. Brass figurines crowded her nightstand: Lord Ganesha on his throne, Shiva and Shakti intertwined, Buddha touching the earth. Next to them, a bottle of Chanel No. 5.

She would sit in a rocking chair in the living room until fatigue overcame her. I helped her back to bed, sliding backward in my sock feet as she shuffled forward facing me. She held my hands like a baby learning to walk. A muffled moan, buried deep in her throat, punctuated each scuff of her feet. We stopped to rest, alone in the house and toe-to-toe in the grief-shrouded hallway.

I searched her Natalie Wood eyes for the woman who'd waited up for teenaged me to come home from dates.

She looked right back. Unflinching attention replaced the morphine stare. I was startled for a beat. And then I leaned toward her, careful to maintain our fragile balance, yet longing to close the space between us. Remnants of our past—harsh words and good intentions—drifted away on our mingled breath.

No longer daughter. No longer mother.

Later, men wearing dark suits wheeled her out of the house, through the living room where my family had gathered, past the rocking chair where Dad sat weeping.

I curled up in the hospital bed, tucking her blankets under my chin. Eternity sung me to sleep, and Chanel No. 5 wafted through my dreams.

A Friend Lay Dying

HER HUSBAND AND I whispered about blood on the toilet paper, and the DNR taped to the refrigerator, and the morphine on the shelf.

From their bedroom, she cried out in pain. He rushed upstairs to her.

I sank onto a footstool, but I longed to race up those stairs behind him.

The house was still.

Already empty.

Stephanie Bryan Died

STEF WAS LYING on the hospital bed in what used to be her dining room. I pulled up a hassock, hoping for one last chat, but disease had carried her beyond conversation. I couldn't interpret her garbled speech, which drifted up through morphine. I stroked her arm, her skin fragile enough to tear. She drifted in and out of sleep, or some place I couldn't follow, just yet. When I rose to leave, I bent close to her ear. "'Bye, Stef. Love you." My fingers lingered on top of her hand, a hand that used to squeeze my shoulder.

Her husband and I held on to each other, before I walked out the front door.

Word came from him too soon. "She's gone."

Today I stand mute at my bedroom window and press my forehead against the glass, as if I might catch a glimpse of her out by the birdbath.

Ten Thousand Things

RAPID-FIRE CAW-CAW-CAW IN the treetops stopped me. I leaned back and shaded my eyes with my hand for a better view. The screeching swelled into rage born of panic. Branches shook, raining leaves. A bird, which I'd expected to be a crow, took off from the branches. But that white underbelly, arms-length wingspan, and effortless flight ... I'll be damned. A hawk.

The crow that I'd heard blasted out of the canopy in pursuit. He dive-bombed the raptor's wing tip. Hawk swerved out of reach. Blackbird screeched, in attack mode, just off the predator's tail. The dogfight shrieked over the sycamores into the distance, shrank to black dots, and disappeared behind rooftops.

Three other crows responded to the distress signal and flapped to the invasion site. Spreading out onto shaky limbs, they screamed warnings into the neighborhood. Hand shading my eyes, I spotted their leader as he returned from the chase. He glided in to join his companions-in-arms. The foliage closed around them, and morning settled into tranquility.

Old tensions eased from my muscles.

Ten thousand things had been screaming at my heart. Middle-eastern refugees drowned at sea, African-Americans murdered in church, Nigerian girls stolen into slavery, Nepal villages buried by earthquake. The news gave me nightmares, but the sky delivered a reminder. The ten thousand things were no more important than the crows that saved their nest today.

Good Bones

"BUY HER PURPLE irises for Mother's Day." Wendy called out a final instruction from her front porch. Wendy read Tarot cards, threw the I Ching, and channeled the voices of mystical guides. She was referring to my stepmom, Mother Kim, who had died a dozen years earlier. Advice about purple irises puzzled me. I'd never mentioned my stepmom's favorite color was purple. And Mother Kim had never mentioned a fondness for irises. Oh, well. I had other things to think about. I was about to buy my first house.

My realtor, Dale, parked her sedan in front of a brick split-level with white shutters. We walked to the stoop. She unlocked the door. "Would you look at that?"

I hurried across the threshold to investigate. The kitchen glowed from the end of the entry hall, ablaze in color. A fiery orange, its brilliance intensified by sunlight streaming through the windows. In this kitchen, a morning cup of coffee would be superfluous. I couldn't help laughing.

Dale pointed out that the sink and countertops needed to be replaced, and there was a hole in the linoleum flooring.

Throughout the house, we encountered design inspired by a 64-pack of crayons. Banana in the family room. Powder blue in the nursery, with white clouds dotting the ceiling. A second bedroom divided horizontally, the walls raspberry from the windowsill to the ceiling, blueberry from midline to floor.

Children had turned the patio into a parking lot for their plastic vehicles. An orange three-wheeler had crashed head-on into the retaining wall that surrounded the terrace. A pink bike with streamers had fallen over on top of a wagon. A playhouse sat in the middle of the yard near the dining room window. I imagined little girls beneath its red roof, fussing at their dolls, under the watchful eyes of their mom. The lawn appeared healthy enough, although it needed mowing. In flowerbeds that bordered the yard on three sides, the leaves of spring bulbs were just breaking ground.

Back inside, I spread my arms. "These colors. They're ... happy."

Dale scowled. "What were they thinking? *Beige* sells." On the other hand, she approved location, price, and construction. "It's got good bones."

I decided to buy the house because it tickled my funny bone.

On a Sunday evening before taking possession, I snuck into the backyard. The owners had moved out; weeds had claimed the lawn. The playhouse was gone, a concrete slab in its place. What would it cost to replace that cement with turf? Could I really afford to remodel the kitchen? Maybe Dale was right about all that color. I collapsed on a stone bench to ponder the scope of the disaster. As I rubbed my temples, wishing someone could reassure me, movement along the fence line caught my attention. The bulbs had bloomed. Hundreds of purple irises were swaying in the breeze.

That's when I realized it was Mother's Day.

Heads I'll Wake Up; Tails I Won't

I WOKE UP this morning, surprised.

Last night I'd fidgeted under the covers. My arm throbbed from shoulder to fingertips in a cross between bee stings and tickling. I gave up on sleep and left my bed to sit on the stairs in the dark. Maybe it's a heart attack. Go to the emergency room. No, what a hassle and expensive, too. Probably pulled a muscle in yoga. Or it's another old-age pain. On the other hand, a throbbing right arm really is a female heart attack symptom. Isn't it?

The edge of the step behind me pressed into my back; mental clamor quieted into a simple question. Which was I willing to do: check in to the emergency room or die in the bedroom?

The latter possibility became absolutely acceptable, because everything I'd known a second earlier fizzled into a stunningly calm No-thing. Devoid of the bedlam I'd labeled concerns, desires, loves, and fears. Preference for life melted away, since there was no longer proof that the thing-called-life had ever existed. Neither was there a preference for this unexpected hush. No-thing felt like ease.

Easy to die. Easy to return to bed, which I did. Heads, I'll wake up. Tails, I won't.

I woke up this morning. Surprised by the toss of the coin.

Ancestor Games

FOR A YEAR, I was intent on building the Downey family tree on a genealogy website. I pored over handwritten census records to verify addresses from a century and a half ago. Clicked to read a birth certificate. Double clicked to study obituaries. Neither eyestrain nor shoulder stress impeded my backward march through history. I filled in our tree back to great-great grandfathers William Benjamin Downey and Daniel Abernathy Brown.

Family stories held that Daniel Brown had died in Missouri. On a day trip across the state in search of Great-Great-Grandpa's gravesite, my husband and I visited two county seats, a local cemetery, and a small-town library. The librarian ended our quest. "Back then families buried their people on farms or in backyards. No official records."

Disappointment dealt a fatal blow to my enthusiasm for the game.

Daniel Abernathy Brown would have been real if I'd placed my hand on his limestone monument, his existence irrefutable had I traced his years with my fingertip.

Perhaps a great-grandniece will pick it up in fifty years. Seeking to identify an empty leaf on the family tree, she'll uncover the name *Dawn Downey*—nothing more than a puzzle piece in her obsession.

Insomnia

WHAT AM I doing awake at . . . oh no . . . four o'clock in the morning? Should be asleep for weeks after that workout at the Y. Maybe I'll get something to eat. Oh, mares eat oats and does eat oats and little lambs eat ivy. May as well meditate. Yeah, yellow will look great in the bathroom. Getting sleepy. Sleepy. Sneezy. Dopey. Sleazy? Don't move. Wow, my face relaxed. That's weird. Nobody gets a tense face. Tense shoulders, maybe. Pl-e-e-e-z, let me go back to sl-e-e-e-p. Cardinal singing. Wonder how to tell if it's a mocking bird, or the bird it's mocking. A kid'll eat ivy, too—.

Asleep, I dream of insomnia.

Recycle

WHEN MY FIRST-GENERATION Kindle arrived, I was too excited to open the box. I danced around the kitchen until I was calm enough to handle scissors. The once-prized e-reader now lies in the bottom of a drawer, replaced twice over. A non-functioning computer cable coils around itself on my closet floor. In the basement, dead boom boxes line a shelf, looking like headstones. On another shelf, a bin filled with telephones and remote controls. Used-up batteries collect inside a plastic bag. Disposal of my previously powered gadgets involves a trek to the electronics recycling center across town ... in the warehouse district ... under the highway ... down by the river ... past the landfill.

Even getting rid of an old spaghetti sauce jar is a five step process. Step one: Set the empty jar on the counter. Step two: (Eventually) plop it into the bottle-and-jar box in the garage. Three: After the carton is full, place it in the car for a trip to the glass-only dumpster in the grocery store parking lot. That used to be the end of it, but we switched grocery stores, which leads to Step Four: Discover the box in the back seat after returning home. Followed by Step Five: Make a special trip to the old grocery store, where the glass-only dumpster is located.

And that is nothing compared to the complications involved in filling a Goodwill box with treasures I used to like, which I claim to have outgrown: shoes, photos, books.

Which in turn is nothing compared to the complexities of

psychological housekeeping. I fill countless therapy sessions and meditation hours rummaging through psychic mementos.

Advice for my loved ones, who'll be left behind to sort the detritus that represented my life: Recycle what's usable. Incinerate what remains—including your memory of me.

Boston Marathon

I CRIED FOR Boston Marathon runners, who suffered traumatic injuries from a terrorist attack. Their loved ones helpless to protect them from the unspeakable. I grieved for the suspects, too. The one died for his cause and the other survived to face our condemnation. Whether he was an all-American college boy radicalized by extremists or an extremist posing as a college boy, my sympathy for him puffed me up with self-congratulation. I rose above automatic hatred.

At church, Pastor Howard led us in prayer. " . . . for the victims and families . . . "

I nodded.

" . . . for the young man being held . . . "

I nodded again, smug in my compassion.

" . . . and for those who would captivate the minds of our young people."

Them too? I hadn't considered the shadowy figures overseas whose influence might have set terror in motion.

Pastor embraces every child as "ours," but my compassion withers under asterisks and exceptions.

Cemetery Song

OUT IN CALIFORNIA, my friend Dawn Moore visited her parents' graves in Forest Lawn. She laughed and cried, reminiscing. I'd like to spread a picnic blanket before my parents' headstones, but Mother and Dad were cremated, their ashes sprinkled into eternity. I wish I could kneel at their monuments.

I'm sorry, Mother. You seldom laughed, and now I understand, now that I'm older than you ever got to be. Do you like my hair?

Look, Dad, here's my latest essay. See, it's funny, just like yours. Please help me with the ending.

But that's only my fantasy.

How do you spread a blanket across eternity?

Dismantled

AFTER TWENTY YEARS of service, our dining room table was stacked in pieces on the curb.

My first husband bought it to fill an empty space in our big new house on the corner. Saturdays, he dusted all the furniture—caressing antique European curves with a 100% cotton cloth dabbed in lemon polish, while the stereo blasted Percy Sledge wailing about how a man loved a woman. We seldom ate at the table. I acquired it in the divorce.

My nephew Anthony, who lived with me after the break-up, slumped over notebooks strewn across the table. His ninth-grade teacher had ordered him to catch up on the year's worth of assignments he'd ignored. I sat opposite, my crossed arms pressed against the unyielding wood. We faced off across an oak no-man's land.

The day Ben and I got married, we extended the table to its full length and pushed it against the wall to make room for a houseful of friends. They covered it with home cooked wedding treats. Over the years, Ben and I ate suppers in front of the television, intertwined on the couch, but when we dined at the table, he waltzed me around the living room for dessert.

We decided to replace the dining room set. But our tired old muscles could not pick that table up, until we discovered the top lifted right off, and the leaves were attached to long arms that slid from underneath a crossbar. It was an engineering marvel, held together by balance. We carried it outside and stacked the pieces on the curb.

The Sherwood Center sent their truck for it. They'll sell it in their thrift store, maybe use the money to purchase school supplies for the autistic children they care for. And soon another family will transform my dismantled memories into a dining room table.

Closure

MY BROTHER MICHAEL said, "A cousin you probably don't remember wants to call you."

"Who?"

"Keisha's mother and Mama were half-sisters."

Mama was a shadow. I hadn't even gone to her funeral. When I was a kid, she often retreated inside herself, her expression turned vacant. The year I was thirteen, she and Dad divorced. Then he remarried and moved away with my siblings and me. It was possible Keisha remembered more about Mama than I did. This newfound cousin might fill in my half-drawn picture.

Michael said, "Our grandfather is Keisha's grandfather, too."

I perked up. I longed to find out about this particular relative, who had died before I was born and whose name I'd never learned. It was as though he'd exploded to life full grown in the 1930s, but there were horror stories. As a little girl, Mama'd adopted a stray kitten; he'd snatched it away and let his hound dogs kill it in front of her. When she'd earned the only high school diploma among his four children, he snarled the paper was as worthless as she was, and he refused to attend the ceremony. He'd cursed her on his deathbed. I didn't know what that meant, but my grandfather sounded like the devil.

Michael asked, "Can I give Keisha your phone number?"

Conversations with my cousin—though still in the future—were already spinning into questions upon mysteries upon riddles.

Was it the specter of our grandfather that had gotten Mama committed? Does his malevolence haunt me, too? Is he the darkness that closes down on me? What stories will Keisha tell?

"Can I give her your number?"

"Yes. Definitely."

Today I'm waiting for Keisha to call. She'll either bring closure ... or suck me into a family inferno.

House on Fire

WILDFIRE SEASON. WITH ten minutes to evacuate after the children were safely in the car, author Terra Trevor snatched up her photo albums. In the years since then, she's lived with the question, "What should I save?"

Carelessly, I fantasize about sacrificing the house in one great immolation that will free me from clutter. Expired grocery lists clone themselves inside my purse. I plow through a closet stuffed with jeans that no longer fit, searching for the single pair that does. Week after week, I crusade to the Salvation Army to cart off boxes filled with last year's fantasies.

What should I save? Rubbish clutters my mind as well as the closets. The same old resentments compete with outdated judgments for the limited space in my consciousness. My personal fire season begins with each new sunrise. Incineration threatens my past, but I refuse to evacuate. Flames licking at my heels, I rush to save treasures. I need that anger I've hoarded for a dozen years. It keeps me warm at night. And one day, I'll dust off the guilt I felt when my closest friendship ended. Guilt is good to have around. And why did I fail to return my brother's call last night? I'll hang on to that—second-guessing always comes in handy.

What should I save? I salvage artifacts from the house-on-fire that is yesterday and drag them to the imaginary safety that tomorrow promises.

For a change, just once, let the house burn down. Let the breeze cool my face, as I stand in the ashes, empty-handed.

January 13, Five AM

1971. A COED scrambles to finish a term paper due in three hours. Her American Lit professor had assigned it six months earlier, but she'd begun writing it only the previous week. Because her father says Cs indicate failure, she maintains a B minus minus minus average at Pomona College. Pizza box. Cigarettes.

1981. A (wannabe) designer manufactures reasons to call in sick. Two years after graduating from the Los Angeles Institute of Fashion Design, she labors in a sweatshop, an hour's commute from her studio apartment in the ghetto. Fabulous wardrobe. Factory job.

1985. A wife (double-income-no-kids) gulps aspirin to tamp down a hangover after the previous night's attempt to anesthetize herself—downing wine at a smoky blues bar. Husband's beer bottle next to her plastic cup, his chair angled away, only the back of his shoulder visible to her. Two-car garage. Credit cards.

2000. A divorcee pauses in her kitchen doorway. She fills a kettle and catches her Mona Lisa refection in the window above the sink. After the pot whistles, her hands close around a steaming mug. Wool sox. Chamomile tea.

2005. A seeker lies on a narrow bed on the final morning of retreat. In the nightlight's glow, yesterday's dharma talk seems to flicker across the ceiling. ... *biggest impediment to clarity is the belief there's an impediment* ... Zafu. Yoga mat.

2011. A woman opens her bedroom window and leans into winter. Above the patio, a half moon hangs in a navy blue sky. The air is bracing, cold against her breasts. It smells like new snow. Wrapped in the gentle snoring that drifts up from her bed, she pads downstairs for breakfast. Bare feet. Birthday oatmeal.

At Home in Paradise

Gravity

I LAY IN bed after waking at 5:00 a.m. Dust was piling up on the ceiling fan blades. I worried about the credit card bill. And why on earth was I lying there, mind wandering? What a waste of time. Tomorrow was going to be different; I'd spring out of bed as soon as my eyes popped open. And then a ray of sun crept across the bedroom wall, and I recalculated my expenses, which brought the credit card under control. As though an alarm had been triggered, I swung my legs from under the covers, mathematical computations replaced by thoughts of raisin bran.

My routine. Day after week after year. Until the day I stopped. As both feet hit the floor on a Thursday morning, it occurred to me ... although I always got up ... I didn't recall *deciding* to get up. There'd been plenty of time to make that decision, but it seemed to be missing.

An experiment followed. I woke at 5:00 a.m. Would my legs swing out of bed by themselves? Or would I lie here feeling foolish until it was time to leave for yoga?

After fluffing the pillow, I settled in. Thoughts flew by like the daily parade at my birdbath. *Boy, that ceiling fan's filthy. Gotta drive Lynn's mom to her doctor's appointment. What if I get lost? Think I'll wash the car. Better wait till next month to buy .... Hold on. What's that?*

I sensed a stirring deep within my interior universe, its location non-specific, but far from any centers of intellectual activity. The

From Dawn to Daylight

impetus to move. As unmistakable as it was undecided. A force other than my volition then swung my legs from under the covers.

Getting up and staying in bed both happened on their own.

I remained perched on the edge of the mattress, still grasping the comforter, wanting to utter a thank you, but unsure where to direct it. It was like discovering that you fall because of gravity, not because you're stupid.

It's obvious only after you see it.

The clock read 6:15. A ray of sun crept across the wall.

Praise the Lord

1. My retirement account is too small to worry about losing.
2. When I go to bed at 8:30, my husband's willing to use headphones while he watches television.
3. My husband refrains from making fun of me when I go to bed at 8:30.
4. I don't need willpower this week, because we polished off the apple pie last week.
5. Telemarketers haven't found my cell phone number yet.
6. There's no way to speed up awakening and no way to slow it down.
7. Dad overruled Mama, and I became Dawn instead of Mabel Geraldine.

History of the Dance

HIGH SCHOOL. BEFORE class began, our modern dance teacher put Blood Sweat and Tears on a turntable in the gym. Their song pulled me to my feet. Freed from the self-consciousness that usually plagued me, I swirled and swayed á la Martha Graham—a spinning wheel that had to go 'round.

Single years. On the dance floor, Stevie Wonder blasting "Living for the City," men mistook my undulation for invitation. Slid their hands downward from my waist. I pushed them back up. They shoved their groins against my belly whenever Barry White moaned. I spun away, learned the rhythms of predator and prey.

Married. My husband pushed the couch against the wall and sang along with Dean Martin ("You're Nobody Till Somebody Loves You") while teaching me to fox trot . . . to follow. His palm pressed the words into my back. His raised arm coaxed me to spin.

A miracle, this dance. I'm led wherever I need to go.

Morning Walk

I MISSED MY walk today. My feet left the house, but I lingered inside my mind—paying the gas bill, shopping for new shoes, composing a grocery list. In my absence, maybe my feet admired the willow around the corner, relished the crunch of broken acorns, and reassured the hound dogs that bayed a warning from behind their fence. My walk ended before I caught up.

At the front door, I chastised myself for all that thinking. I reached for the doorknob, along with the promise of greater attention tomorrow.

A cardinal whistled, reminding me that tomorrow . . . nothing needs to change. And everything will.

Breakfast for Four at the Silent Retreat

A CHAIR IS pushed away from our table, the cushioned seat still bearing an imprint. The aroma of coffee hangs in the air over an empty cup.

Opposite me, a woman crunches a salad. Her wrinkled hands look like they're accustomed to garden soil and dishwater. Inexplicably, I want to make her laugh.

On my left, another companion sips from a water glass. When she sets it down, it thuds against the table. She wields her fork with clanky stabs.

I lean over a mug of tea, breathe in licorice and peppermint. As steam seeps into my pores, the cool taste of mint surprises my tongue.

In the Presence of Love

I RACED THROUGH the kitchen, shouted over my shoulder toward the upstairs office where my husband was bent over his computer. "I love you." On the threshold into the garage, I reached to pull the door closed, but stopped. My eyes watered and I felt a catch in my throat, my body calling me back from the errand that had seemed imperative just a second before, calling me home to stand in the presence of Love.

In a tiny room that smelled of oil and garbage, rakes and shovels mounted like artwork on the walls, floor carpeted with dried leaves, Love introduced Itself to me. And it was not the companionship nor sweet embraces wrapped inside a marriage, but a force of nature that flooded my pores, uprooted my plans, and spilled over my banks in tears.

Winter Blues

WELL PAST SUNRISE—don't keep responsibilities waiting, Dawn.

I brushed my teeth, mint tingling my taste buds. And then I paused at the bedroom window to reconsider my commitment to the day.

Storms had buried our patio under white powder and sculpted hoary mounds atop planters. The skeleton of a rose bush danced in the wind. Our deck umbrella hung in frozen folds impervious to the bluster that had overturned my husband's hammock. It seemed impossible anyone had ever rested there. Birches stretched peeling spines toward heaven, as their branches reached out across the yard, abandoned by robins, sparrows, cardinals, and jays. I mourned the absence of their morning chatter.

I slumped back to bed, but winter stalked me there, too, robbing me of sleep. Like a cold breath down my neck, an air current from the furnace sneaked under the blankets. I wrapped covers around me tight as a mummy; still, I shivered. The comforter offered no comfort.

Yard Work/Yard Play

MS. FASTIDIOUS NEIGHBOR, astride a lawn tractor, circled the ash tree in her front yard, mulching. Periodically she climbed off to stuff leaves into yard bags. Her mower droned all morning, until she'd transformed copper-colored carpet into a field of emerald that stretched from the street to her front door. Brimming yard waste bags stood in an obedient triangle at the end of her driveway.

How I envied that perfection.

Next morning my husband helped her re-fill those sacks, then marched through our front door. He shook his head. "Last night somebody plowed their car straight into her bags." He scowled. Grunted. "Teenagers."

I pursed my lips. Lifted an eyebrow. Imagined sighting those bags in my headlights.

The decision.

The impact.

The shower of leaves.

Strike!

Teenagers. How I envied them.

Gardening vs. Yard Work

I'M JEALOUS OF Cheryl Wilfong, who teaches meditation over in Vermont. Cheryl has a Garden. In which she gardens. In which she is mindful. Her Garden rewards her with the scent of lilac.

Here in Missouri, I've got The Yard. In which I work. In which I sweat, stink, and break my nails.

The Yard doesn't care. It lies around in a self-indulgent sprawl. It gobbles the food I put on its table. Guzzles a big gulp, while refusing to clean up its room. It spits out crabgrass and chickweed.

(Mindful of my resentment) I'd like to ship The Yard to Cheryl. Maybe it will sprout some cooperation, if she teaches it to meditate.

Swept Away

WHEN SPRING TEMPERATURES soared to sixty, I ventured onto the patio.

My pots bore the corpses of last summer's annuals, and milkweed competed with dandelions and thatch where there ought to be grass, and my hoses sprawled in muddy tangles, and our ground cover (cultivated from ivy sprigs out of Julie's yard, although she warned me against the idea) sneaked under the neighbor's fence and . . . .

In the film, *Into Great Silence*, a monk sweeps a monastery walkway. The seasons pass. He rakes leaves, shovels snow, and in the spring, he sweeps again. Doesn't suffer. Sweeps.

Lost in great noise, I suffer.

Inside the Flu

THE PILLOWCASE, OR maybe it's your hair, scratches the back of your neck, but the pain that stabs your shoulder—as it yanks attention away from the muscle spasm squeezing your back like a full-body mammogram—prevents you from reaching up to make an adjustment. Besides, with the slightest twitch, shivers rattle your bones and race across your skin, even underneath two down comforters, a fleece jacket, tee shirt, sweat pants, and wool socks. Anyway, lift an arm, while you simultaneously hold a thermometer steady under your tongue? Impossible.

Less Worry. More Food.

THE REFRIGERATOR WAS bulging. We'd stuffed crab legs into the deli bin; they were a gift from family. Then Ben had come home after his Saturday breakfast with Victor, bearing goodies from Farmer's Market: a bushel of pears, roasted chickens, three heads of romaine, fishes and loaves, and I think an entire banana tree.

The day before, the fridge had been a food desert.

Oh, I'd been thinking about going to the store. I'd written a list. Researched recipes. Budgeted. Scheduled. Cleaned the kitchen to make way for all that potential food. Boy, was I busy with my visit to the grocer. But I cannot decipher any connection between my raising of all that dust and the transformation of our refrigerator into a cornucopia.

Is this happening with the laundry, too? I fuss and worry and fidget, and then one morning dirty clothes end up in the washer, while my mind is off working on an entirely different problem.

Our California vacation came off in the same mysterious manner. One minute I was saying, "Honey, I'd like to—" and the next minute Kate Guendling was dropping us at the airport.

I'm inclined to experiment with this. Strategize less. Let the doing happen when it's ready.

California Redwoods

AFTER MY HUSBAND, sister, and I paid our admission fee at Santa Barbara Botanic Garden, we strolled down a manicured pathway through tableaus of native plants. Michelle led us to her favorite bench opposite a stand of redwoods squeezed into a natural habitat, like giraffes at the zoo.

Ben and I pulled off Highway 1 to worship in the shade of another grove of the California giants. The trees loomed skyward, blocking out all but a pinpoint of blue. A stream trickled past our feet, its gurgle a hymn that barely broke the sacred quiet.

In Napa Valley, a winery tour guide told us the Korbel Brothers had cleared redwoods to plant champagne grapes. Stumps had clung to the ground for decades, proving impossible to remove. When a television show requested use of the vineyard for a location shoot to film explosions, the Korbels said sure, as long as they blew up those pesky stumps.

How to describe the redwood. Zoo animal? Temple god? Cannon fodder?

Or simply tree?

Gratitude for Ugly

"BET THE OCEAN'S just around the next bend. I can smell it." Ben was driving us north on Highway 1, just past San Luis Obispo. We climbed through foothills parched brown from drought.

I strained against the seat belt to peer around him. "Seems like we should have gotten there by now."

One more loop and the landscape opened like parting curtains. On with the show. Gulls screamed a soundtrack. The Pacific shimmered green under the afternoon sun. "Beautiful!" We rounded another curve; whitecaps crashed against cliffs. "Oh my gosh." A hairpin turn revealed a lighthouse perched on a spit in a fairy tale tableau. "Wow." A whale lolled and dove like a ballerina. "Holy cow." Hour after hour, the scenery unfolded, too grand for photos, too dazzling for words.

The hills closed around us again, miles of beige. The car engine droned. I flipped through a tourist guidebook, which offered enticements down the road.

Without warning the beach reappeared. Seals dotted sun-bleached rocks. Waves crashed. Pelicans dived. "Look at that."

Good thing God stuck some ugly in there so I'd appreciate gorgeous.

Me, Myself, and I

I AWOKE RELUCTANTLY, weighed down by the burden of drawing breath. I was devoid of ambition. No unresolved problem spurred me into action. No unmet need beckoned. No impending disaster threatened. Life felt completed, if not content. My disposition flatlined at *let me be done with it.*

But the bruising pressure of the mattress against my spine wailed more insistently than the death wish. I shuffled downstairs for aspirin to ease the nagging in my back and then returned to the bedroom, slipped back under the covers, and waited.

The pain reliever's caffeine cleared the clouds from my imagination. My equilibrium creaked back to center; blood, bones, and breath became as inviting as the void that stretched beyond them.

The Dawns—pre- and post-caffeine—seemed real, as though I might be trapped inside one or the other. Their story lines (one tragedy, the other romantic comedy) ran parallel, as relentless as railroad tracks.

But how could they qualify as real, if an insignificant aspirin snapped them into and out of existence? How is it possible a tiny white pill turned them into dandelion puffs borne on the winds of eternity?

Me and *Myself* have questions, which *I* declines to answer.

Parkville Imagined

IN APRIL, THE river beckoned. I strolled my favorite path in Parkville. The Missouri swept along beside the trail. Silent, swift, and steady. Snags flew downstream. A sand barge chugged along in the opposite direction. I rested on a bench and puzzled over a patch of dandelions, their tenacity admirable in the park and hateful in my yard. But that was spring, before the storms howled through, before the river poured over the landscape.

Come July, I lost my bearings. A lake appeared where I'd last seen my landmarks. Either the river had transformed the setting, or I had only imagined the trail, the bench, the dandelions ... and April.

City Girl Makes Peace with Nature:

Lesson Three

I SIT CROSS-LEGGED on a ridge two hundred feet above the Illinois River. A jagged rock pokes my ankle, while my bare arms welcome the summer breeze. On the water's surface, sunlight plays with shadows cast by passing clouds. I close my eyes to meditate, the river disappearing into the midnight behind my lids. Pine scents the humid air. Wisps of laughter float by. I peek. A raft is drifting downstream, its occupants specs of confetti at the bottom of the bluff. After an on oak leaf flies off a branch, it swirls downward, until an updraft reverses its direction. It lands in a cottonwood that towers above me.

A river disappears.

Confetti laughs.

A leaf falls up.

Today's lesson: trust.

Avian Enchantment

I FIRST SUSPECTED the existence of a magical world last spring, when I passed beneath the branches of an oak and heard birds roosting above my head. I tried to get a good look at the warblers, but no amount of twisting or squinting rendered them visible. Chirping emanated from everywhere and nowhere at once; I spread my arms and let the chatter rain down on me, grinning at the enchantment in the canopy.

After my husband installed a bird feeder outside our kitchen window, an overpopulated city sprang to life in our silent winter garden. As I pressed my forehead against the frigid pane, great clouds of birds swooped in to feed in a jittery mass and then exploded off their perch like scattershot. I was a child again, watching a magician wave his hankie. Voilá, a flock appears. Voilá, it vanishes.

We ventured into a feed store redolent of cedar. We were explorers who'd crossed a border into foreign territory. The owner spoke a language peppered with exotic words like milo, while she rang up a fifty-pound bag of seeds and a bird book for identifying our backyard population.

Today a visitor clad in polka-dotted plumage flapped onto the feeder tray. I scoured the book for its photo in order to prove its existence. When I looked up, the traveler had vanished, along with the magic.

Too-Tight Jeans

AFTER SNACKING MY way through the holidays, I suspected the cause for the contortions required to pull on my jeans. So, while the doctor was treating Hubby for a pulled muscle, I stepped onto the scale. The digital read-out shaped itself into a number. 146.

"Holy shit!"

The doctor chuckled. "That's what everybody says in January."

I followed Ben to the parking lot. "We will not be eating again until March."

"Yes, Dear."

"I'm going to search your car for contraband snacks."

"Yes, Dear."

"We're heading to the Y as soon as we get home."

"Yes, Dear."

Panic fizzled before we pulled into our garage. In the past, panic had led to the flip side of beauty-angst: *screw it; I'm going to eat what I want; who cares, anyway.* This time an unfamiliar sensation enveloped me: calm.

I replayed the scene in the doctor's office. Anxiety had arisen after I'd stepped onto the scale, but I had not gained weight in the seconds just before. Therefore, responsibility for my unhappiness must lay elsewhere. The culprit—those scratch marks, which I'd interpreted as "146." Aka Failure. Ugly. Unacceptable.

The holidays were past, and my food intake would return to normal. My established treadmill/yoga routine would continue.

My body would shrink to its pre-Thanksgiving size.

And yet nothing would change until I read another set of scratches on another scale.

Washing Dishes at the Silent Retreat

KATE, OUR TEACHER, assigned the eight of us to work together cleaning the kitchen after meals and to complete the task in silence. One by one, other women pushed back their chairs, then rose to take a shift at the sink. The slowest eater, I lingered over honeyed quinoa, kale sweet potato stew, and gluten-free brownies. By the time I swallowed a last bite, there was very little cleaning left. In the meantime, Annette whisked away dirty plates, washed, rinsed, dried, put away, and swept up crumbs, her freshly shampooed hair perfuming the air near my shoulder.

On day three she retired to the living room without stopping at the sink. Oh, dear. Kate must have instructed her to relax, because Some People were not helping. Some People were lollygagging. I felt their hot eyes on me. I heard their silent screaming judgments. Embarrassed, I hurried through my dinner, then scrubbed pans and dried flatware.

At retreat's end, Annette announced she'd interrupted (without prompting from Kate) her age-old habit of assuming responsibility for all the work. She'd been shocked that chores were completed without her help.

Perhaps at the next retreat, I'll interrupt my old habit of mind reading.

What Do You Want?

YESTERDAY MORNING, AS I awakened next to my husband, if you'd asked me what I wanted most in the world, the answer would have come on a contented sigh. "Nothing at all. What more could I possibly want?"

Ha.

Yesterday afternoon, my yoga buddy pulled up to class in a white convertible. I wanted that.

I want to stand in front of Mona Lisa at the Louvre, see what all the fuss is about. Sit next to *Vogue's* editor at every show during New York Fashion Week. I want paparazzi to follow me around.

I want to lie on the couch in my pajamas, watching movies until I'm eighty-five.

I lust for a live-in hair stylist, because dreadlocks require more care than I'd planned on. I crave maid service. And a loft in the city. And a John Deere mini-excavator.

I want to sing back-up for my sister Michelle, ask Uncle Al what he regrets, become the next great stand-up comic, and deliver a bring-down-the-house Academy Awards acceptance speech.

I want to cradle a newborn baby.

Win the Indy 500.

Another breath, another want. It exhausts me. Let me fade into the real, free from my desires. Even wanting that, I'm still enslaved.

So-Called Problems

EMAILS. PHONE CALLS. Deadlines. My problems were too big for their britches. I hauled them to the car and drove to my favorite park, a strip of flood plain sandwiched between the river and the railroad tracks. I parked, opened the windows. An air horn blasted. The ground shook. An eastbound Burlington Northern thundered through a crossing. The engine labored against its mile-long string of cars, loaded with coal from the mines of Montana. Just ahead, the Missouri River crawled toward St. Louis. I let the wind breathe for me. It carried my so-called problems off into the unconcerned clouds.

Trite or Truth?

1. A rising tide lifts all boats.
2. Beauty is in the eye of the beholder.
3. Ashes to ashes, dust to dust.
4. Here today, gone tomorrow.
5. I haven't got a penny to my name.
6. I wasn't born yesterday.
7. The lights are on but nobody's home.

Alzheimer's Duet

AT THE NURSING home, in my role as a hospice volunteer, I knocked on the door of 316.

Bessie peeked out, her face set in question marks until ancient eyes sparked recognition, and she embraced me like her long lost child. "It's been a while since you've stopped by."

"Yes, a whole week," I said.

"Sit down, dear. How long has it been since I saw you?"

"Way too long. A whole week."

Whose Voice was that, responding to questions as though they'd never been asked before? Where was my usual catch of impatience?

"How long has it been since you were here?"

"A whole week. Can you believe it?"

A sublime duet. One could not control dementia. The other could not control the Voice.

At Home in Paradise

I WOKE BEFORE dawn, blanket wrapped around my ankles in a serpentine tangle. My husband snored beside me. Intent on straightening covers, I wriggled from underneath his arm, but a silver glow that peeked from the edges of the blind drew me from bed. After opening the window to let autumn cool my aching shoulder, I pressed my forehead against cold glass. Denuded by November wind, birches swayed in the moonlight, and their fallen leaves rustled as they skipped across our patio. An airplane roared above the night. I shuffled back to bed, the scent of an apple core on the nightstand beating a counterpoint to body odor from long-past-laundry-day sheets. Still asleep, my husband wrapped his arm around me once again.

The Inheritance

Sample chapter from *Stumbling Toward the Buddha: Stories about Tripping over My Principles on the Road to Transformation*

The Inheritance

DAY ONE. I was either trying to outrun my history—or catch up with it.

I sat by myself in a college student lounge, waiting for the Santa Barbara Writers Conference to convene. Tension knotted my shoulders as other would-be authors filed in, meandered toward the registration table, and settled in overstuffed chairs. Avoiding eye contact, I scanned the room for familiar faces. *Did they know Dad? Is that one of his students? Will anyone remember me?*

I'd grown up in Santa Barbara and then moved away. I hadn't returned in the ten years since my parents had died. Dad was a local hero. He'd taught at this conference for twenty years. He'd also published five books, authored 500 newspaper columns, and taught creative writing to 7,000 Santa Barbarans.

In the meantime, I had limped through high school and college, and then dabbled in the careers of school librarian, fashion designer, hotel manager, university counselor, and hospital administrator. I'd resigned from the last position to become a writer.

Along the way there were clues to an eventual love affair with the written word. As an undergrad, I preferred the essay question to the multiple-choice, the term paper to the final exam. Graduate school brought insight and the stirrings of a voice. My first research paper earned an A+ from my M.A. advisor. He added the comment, "You don't know how good you are." I flirted with prose in every job: sculpted memos into works of art, transformed newsletters into novels, reviewed dance productions for the hometown paper, and even proofed copy for classifieds. But I didn't notice the pattern. Like a haughty cheerleader pursued by the captain of the chess team, I didn't know *writing* existed until the day I ran away with it.

I quit my job to follow in Dad's footsteps. He would have disapproved.

I'm forty-one. After sojourns in Portland, St. Louis and Minneapolis, I've landed in Kansas City. I've found the perfect job, and call my parents to share the news

"Dad, guess what?" He barely gets in a "Hi, Tootie" before I launch into my story. I pause for his congratulations.

He coughs from advancing lung disease. "I don't know why you keep quitting, but this job sounds good. I guess you're failing up."

I laugh along with him, but my cheeks burn, because I can't tell if he's praising me or mocking me.

CNN drones behind his wheezing.

Day Two. The leader of the morning workshop—a Fred Astaire type—stacked papers and books on a table at the front of the room. He wore sharply creased trousers and a crisp oxford shirt, with a cardigan draped across his shoulders. After introducing himself to the class, he strolled toward me. I averted my gaze from his face to the floor. His loafers advanced, stopping just opposite my sandals. I peeked at his knees, glanced at his belt buckle, and finally looked into his eyes.

He took my hand in both of his. "They told me you were coming. Your papa was a dear, dear friend. I miss him."

The breath I was holding escaped in a sigh. "Thank you. Me, too."

I'm twenty-eight, home for the holidays. My teen-aged sister and I are feuding. She sweeps past me to greet other family members with effusive air kisses. Wherever she stands, she turns her back to me. Her haughtiness reduces me from career woman to kindergarten victim.

After a day of toughing it out, I confide in Dad. We stand outside the front door. The night-blooming jasmine he'd planted along the driveway gleams in the moonlight. I tell him I'd rather spend Christmas with friends than endure that little shit's silent treatment.

"I wish you'd stay," he says. "You're not a quitter. I don't call you Snake Bite for nothing."

It's the only time he's called me Snake Bite. He opens the door to encourage me back into the house. The scents of pine and cinnamon fill the living room. Seduced by this flirtation with his approval, I follow Dad inside and stay for Christmas.

Day Three. I broke the silence.

Other writers read their work aloud and endured the critiques. Their hands shook and their voices halted, while I hunkered down in the back of the room.

They'll find out I'm a fraud.

I imagined Dad's colleague embarrassed to discover his dear friend's daughter had no talent. When Mr. Fred Astaire read my name from his sign-up sheet, I interpreted his wry smile and the ironic lilt in his voice as *we'll just see what you can do, missy.*

I stood in front of the class and read an essay. The group was supposed to offer suggestions, but no one spoke. I looked up from the page. They applauded. I gasped. It seemed polite to murmur thank you, but I wanted the clapping to stop. Surely I'd get into trouble for breaking some rule.

The teacher held up his copy of my composition. "You see," he said in that same clever tone, an eyebrow raised. "She did everything I told you to do in creative nonfiction."

From Dawn to Daylight

I did? How did that happen?

The afternoon session had already begun by the time I located it on the sprawling campus. At first the room looked empty. The chairs had been pushed back against the walls, forming a semicircle that faced a stool labeled the Hot Seat. One after another, participants perched there, read a work-in-progress, and listened to their colleagues' evaluations.

The facilitator directed the proceedings from behind a bare wooden desk. Reading glasses perched halfway down her nose emphasized her deadpan expression. After the class discussed chapter one of a memoir and the latest draft of a how-to manual, she tapped her roster with a pencil. "Dawn Downey is next."

Oh no, not me. My face grew hot and my hands cold, but I clutched my papers and stood.

I'm twenty. I stand at the sink, washing dishes. Dad sits at the kitchen table. He slouches in the chair with his legs stretched out. His size-twelve feet block the doorway. He studies my report card, which he holds in one hand, and then looks at me over his glasses. "You're failing."

"No I'm not. They're Cs, not Fs."

"Watch your mouth." His voice is low. It rumbles through the kitchen.

I scour away at nonexistent grime in a skillet until Dad stalks out of the room.

The Hot Seat vibrated with menace. I willed my rubbery legs to move and crossed the expanse as though wading through waist-high mud. When I'd reached the middle of the room, a booming voice broke the silence.

"Dawn Downey? Bill's daughter? We lived up the street when you were in high school."

I turned to locate the source. A shout from the opposite corner rang out. "Bill's daughter? God, I loved that old man. I took his class six times."

The instructor frowned. She took off her spectacles. "Downey. I should have recognized the name. Your dad is the reason I'm here."

They converged on me. They hugged and patted and kissed. Their affection quelled my internal voices, which criticized and second-guessed. After cowering in the shadows for a lifetime, I basked in this newfound celebrity.

Order was restored, and I took my place on the Hot Seat. When I finished my recitation, someone yelled out, "You can't stop there. I've got to know what happens next."

The instructor held up her hand to prevent me from responding. "You'll just have to buy her book. Excellent work."

Maybe I *could* be a writer.

I'm eighteen. Dad drops me off at the Greyhound station. The brick building looms in front of me like Mount Doom. A bus labeled "Los Angeles" idles nearby. Exhaust blackens the air and stings my lungs.

I'm returning to college after a weekend at home spent begging my parents to let me quit. When they refuse, I plead for a year off, and then a semester.

College life suffocates me. The co-ed dorms force me into unwanted intimacy with men I don't know. Stodgy literature professors suck the energy from Hemingway. The social pressure cooker that is 1970s affirmative action pits privileged white students from the suburbs against un-privileged black students from the inner city. As a middle class black girl, I'm trapped between the two factions.

Dad sends me back to a world where I'm lost, but his eyes are misty when he kisses me goodbye.

His tears embarrass me, as though I've accidentally seen him naked.

Day Four. I strained to hear my neighbor's voice above the din in the crowded cafeteria. Three of us had walked to lunch together and took places at one end of a rectangular table. A group of women we hadn't met took the remainder of the seats. They appeared to be conference staff, judging from the number of people vying for their attention. Snippets of their conversation broke through the surrounding racket. " . . . sales figures for my book." " . . . find the time to write my column." " . . . have to call my agent back." They represented everything I aspired to be. Popular, polished, published.

One of them picked up her chair and squeezed it in beside mine. "If it wasn't for your father, I wouldn't be a writer."

We sat knee to knee. As she leaned in to me, the noisy room receded. There was only the intensity of her gaze and the sweetness of her memory.

"When I came here as a student," she said, "I was scared to death. I took your dad's workshop because I heard he was friendly. On the last day, he asked, 'When are we going to hear from you?' I was too nervous to read my own work, but he talked me into it. I walked to the front of the room, shaking, close to tears. He leaned over and whispered, 'You're safe here.' And he held my hand while I read."

I was spellbound. We sat wordlessly for a few seconds. Our mingled breath held her story aloft like a feather. As it floated away, she rose and returned to her colleagues and to the anonymity of clanking plates and peeling laughter.

He'd held her hand while she read.

A stranger had just revealed that my father was Superman, and his secret power was tenderness. Maybe, if I'd known his identity before he'd died, Superman would have held my hand, too.

I'm sixteen. Dad and I huddle with his boss, the editor of the Santa Barbara News-Press. Our three chairs form a tight circle.

I propose an article for the paper: race relations among high school students. I rattle off prospective interview questions for my classmates. I read my synopsis, stumbling over the power of the two men beside me. Intimidation halts my speech. Excitement propels me.

The editor nods while I talk. He smiles at me, then turns to Dad. "What do you think, Bill?"

Dad folds his hands in his lap. "I wish I'd heard about it before now."

His words press in on my chest. I freeze. "Sorry, Dad." My heart races. I study my feet. "Sorry."

I feel him next to me like a rock face I can't possibly scale.

The editor's comments drift by. "Flesh it out." "Meet again." They grow fainter as the room fades away and I disappear.

Day Five. Dad's former students caught up with me as I entered buildings, emerged from restrooms, and strolled down walkways. Messengers from my father, they shared the words of encouragement he'd written across their manuscripts. Some had continued to meet for a decade after Dad's death, reserving an empty seat for him at the head of the table. They recited his pithy advice. "Take more risks." "Write outrageously." They repeated phrases unfamiliar to my ears. "I'm proud of your progress." "Just incredible." They unveiled my inheritance: Dad's Technicolor self-portrait, which I'd only seen in black and white.

I'm ten years old, lying in the bow of his cabin cruiser. We've been fishing, just the two of us. He sits on the deck smoking his pipe. Vin Scully is calling a Dodgers game on the radio. Mosquitoes buzz; lightning bugs flicker. The river rocks me to sleep.

Day Six. I juggled a plate of fruit and a glass of orange juice as I navigated around the buffet table at the closing brunch. Suitcases, backpacks, and tote bags left little space for walking. The ballroom resounded with shouted compliments and promises to email. There were flurries of exchanged business cards.

After finishing the meal, we settled in for an awards ceremony. Each announcement of someone else's accomplishment stabbed me with a sense of failure and then guilt for my lack of generosity. The inner turmoil distracted me, until the sound of the family name yanked my attention back. " . . . Downey . . . first prize . . . creative nonfiction." A tablemate poked me in the ribs, another squeezed my shoulders, assuring me I'd heard correctly. My cheeks ached from grinning as I made my way to the stage.

I'm six years old. Dad sits on the step stool in the kitchen, holding a jar of pickled pigs' feet. I climb onto his lap. His big arms surround me as he reaches into the jar and offers me a bite. The tangy taste plays hopscotch on my tongue. Dad grins. I swing my legs.

When I reached the stage, the conference founder presented me with a certificate and kissed me on the forehead. I read the essay aloud at the pace of chocolate melting in my mouth. I savored this bit of success at the craft Dad loved. The spotlight's glow made up for all the years I'd felt invisible. When I took my bow, students whom my father had encouraged and teachers he had taught applauded my achievement. They nodded their approval. Invisible arms wrapped around me, and I knew Dad's hand held mine.

I'm fifty-four. My father beams. "Incredible, Snake Bite, just incredible."

Apple Pie for Two

Sample chapter from the forthcoming *Searching for My Heart: Essays About Love*

Apple Pie for Two

I WIPED THE butter off the laptop and then reveled in the aroma of cinnamon that filled my astonished kitchen.

My husband burst through the door. "Something smells delicious in here."

Grinning, I could hardly get the words out. "Baked you a present, Honey."

An apple pie cooled on the counter, in direct rebuttal to the fact I hated cooking and wasn't even that crazy about eating.

Ben clapped his hand to his chest. "Oh, my god. It's beautiful."

It was. A golden volcano with juice seeping through its fissures and steam escaping its peak. The dish exceeded my culinary skills. I'd attempted it partly because Ben had mentioned he loved homemade apple pie, but mostly because he didn't expect it. He had cheered every uninspired meal set in front of him. His patience had engendered both my gratitude and bravery.

"You did this for me?" he asked.

The question hung in the air between us. I savored it.

There was nothing to savor about the food I'd grown up with. My father caught catfish in the days when sophisticated palates scorned it as a bottom feeder. He hunted squirrel, coon, duck, and beaver, accompanied by hounds that were breadwinners rather than pets. Mama baked the coon with barbeque sauce—

a failed attempt to disguise the scavenger's bitter taste. Potatoes and carrots swam around it in a puddle of grease.

In the summer, she picked dandelion greens out of our yard and rutabagas that grew back by the alley. As I picked alongside her, Des Moines' hard-packed clay soil dug into my knees, while mosquitoes tormented a thin-skinned spot above my elbow. I knelt for hours; it seemed a mountain of raw greens cooked down to only a slimy spoonful. Sometimes corn-on-the-cob appeared in our kitchen, sacks full of it. Sweet corn tasted like a reward, but shucking it was punishment, especially for me, squeamish about the worms that lurked beneath the silk.

About once a year, Mama baked fudge. Blocks of it, heavy as bricks, sat in the icebox wrapped in waxed paper. She doled out tiny chunks to us kids. It was hard and cold against my front teeth when I bit into a slice. With six in the family, everyone nursing a voracious sweet tooth, the fudge disappeared after a day or two. Dad claimed the bulk of it. When Mama fixed another of Dad's favored treats, he didn't have to share. Nobody else liked chitlins—pig intestines, which she washed in the kitchen sink, then boiled all day long. Their stench dug claws into my throat and lungs. The house stank for weeks.

Toiling over stove and sink, Mama was borne around the kitchen on a tide of hardscrabble routine, which crowded out any notion of teaching her little girl how to cook. I perched on a step stool in the corner, absent any desire to learn. In those days, want—whether the object was Mama's attention, a new doll, or an extra piece of fudge—got you nowhere.

Dad and Mama divorced the year I turned twelve. He married Kim Carol, who preferred poetry and metaphysics to the culinary arts. Concerned about my lethargy, she took me to a doctor, who confirmed low blood sugar. The doctor explained my new relationship with food—eat every three hours every day—as though he were prescribing antibiotics. Mother Kim found no joy in cooking and didn't help search for recipes that would benefit my health. By the time she entered my life, I had already absorbed subliminal messages from Mama that only the wife fixed the family meals. When Mother Kim relegated me to salad making, my kitchen education stagnated at rinsing lettuce and washing dishes.

Meanwhile, she struggled to maintain the Elizabeth Taylor figure of her twenties. Sweets were banned. Tab replaced Kool-Aid. When I was in college, she warned if my thighs developed saddlebags, I'd never get rid of them. She cajoled me to join her in fad diets. Her mantra, "We'll lose five pounds this weekend."

During the years spent with Mama, meal preparation was synonymous with forced labor. Mother Kim did nothing to dissuade me from that view, and in fact, after she came into my life, food became a bitter pill.

I found the apple pie recipe online at a blog called *Food Wishes: Video Recipes with Chef John*. His initial instruction, "peel and core the apples," tightened my mouth into a grimace. The words fell through a hole in my chest, a space where other women stored cooking lessons learned from mom.

Surely Chef John would glare out from the computer screen, the way Mother Kim had during my first visit home as a married woman. When I'd hesitated at the stove, her impatience had wilted me, "You can't even make gravy? How in the world do you feed your husband?"

Here's how. I sat at my kitchen table with *The Joy of Cooking*, a dictionary, and three tablets. I flipped the cookbook open to the beef chapter, read through a recipe until an unfamiliar word, like *braise*, popped up. Looked up *braise* in the dictionary. If it sounded do-able, I returned to the recipe, copied all the ingredients, including measurements, onto a grocery list—tablet number one. When the recipe required an unusual utensil, like a roasting pan, I listed that on tablet number two (after looking it up in the dictionary). Next, a perusal of the chicken chapter, followed by fish, casseroles, and vegetables. On tablet number three, the days of the week. Beside each day, a menu. At the grocery store, I studied labels to determine which size of block cheese would produce half a cup shredded. Gadgets required a stop at Target on the way home. And what distinguished a spatula from a pancake turner? I repeated the process every week, because my cupboards held none of the essentials. Staples? They fastened papers together.

I pushed play on Chef John's video. The camera focused on his hands, a knife in one, an apple in the other. He cut off the ends, and then peeled around. "I don't have any tricks for that. Just use a paring knife. You can use a peeler." He cut the fruit in quarters and then sliced off the cores. "I'm not a big corer. I don't have one of those things you push through. Actually I think I do have one, but it's rusty."

What did he say? I pushed rewind. "… use a paring knife … " and then "…one of those things you push through." Chef John dismissed gadgets as optional. I wanted to kiss him.

I studied the comments below the typed recipe. Question: *Won't the bottom crust be soggy?* Chef responded, "I've never really thought about it." Question: *Forgot to dot the apples with butter. Will it be okay?* Chef responded, "Should be okay." Question: *What about store-bought crusts?* Response, "Just fine." *How do you get the first piece of pie out?* "It might fall apart. That's normal."

I practically memorized the recipe, comments, and video—determined to root out deception. Desperate to identify any turn of a phrase that, misunderstood, would lead to humiliation. My faith grew. Let Chef John hold my hand; I would end up with pie.

"'Bye, Honey. See you tonight." After Ben left the house for the day, I set up my laptop on the kitchen counter. The tinkle of Oscar Peterson's mellow jazz piano floated from our CD player. Apple peel ribbons dropped into the sink. Knife clacked against cutting board. "Ow." I knocked my forehead against an open cabinet door, rubbed the sore spot with a sticky hand. That's okay, keep going. The counter turned white from spilled cornstarch and sugar. I stirred—*damn, is it too wet?* Rewound the video. "… going to be really juicy," Chef John said. An errant peel squished underfoot. I poured the goopy mixture into a crust-lined pie plate, popping a slice into my mouth. Crunchy and sweet. For heaven's sake—delicious. But too many apples, the top crust will never fit. Checked the video again. My concoction matched the freeze frame of Chef John's unbaked pie. The top crust broke when I eased it on. No problem. Pinch it together. I painted the whole thing with beaten egg in careless swipes, just like Chef. Hot air hit my face when I opened the oven door to slide the pie inside.

I had just wiped off the laptop screen and was blowing sugar from the keyboard when our motorized garage door announced Ben's arrival.

He burst into the kitchen. "Something smells delicious in here."

Snapping the computer shut, I pointed to the pie. "Made you a present, Honey."

From Dawn to Daylight

"Oh, my god. Apple?" His forward momentum halted, but his gaze remained fixed on the treat, as though I might snatch it away if he blinked. "You did this for me?"

The first piece out of the pan fell apart. That was normal.

I presented him a saucer heaped with apples, juice, and crust. After scooping up a forkful, he closed his eyes to emphasize the *mmmm.*

"Yes, for you," I said. "For both of us."

Acknowledgements

The author gratefully acknowledges the following publications where essays first appeared, in slightly different form:

Kansas City Voices: A Periodical of Writing and Art: "The Inheritance"
Skirt! Magazine: "Good Bones"
The Best Times: "Too Young for Old Age"

Thank you to loved ones and colleagues who added their gifts to this book.

Developmental editor/coach, Marcia Meier

Copyeditor/steadfast cheerleader, Julie Tenenbaum

WTF Writers Group: Jessica Conoley, who knows where stories begin and end; Annie Raab, who says "make it more tangible," and Dane Zeller, who prods me to clarify what the story's about.

Brenda Miller, author of *The Pen and the Bell: Mindful Writing in a Busy World.* Her essays set the standard I aspire to.

Cheryl Wilfong, author of *The Meditative Gardener: Cultivating Mindfulness of Body, Feelings, and Mind.* Her blog is an ongoing source of inspiration.

Terra Trevor, for suggesting a reading list that has improved my writing.

Dawn Moore, who knows what I'm trying to say and laughs in the right places.

Uncle Al (Allen Downey, Sr.), for reading my essays as fast as I can publish them and always offering compliments.

My sister, Michelle Downey Lawyer, who told me to write with confidence.

And a special thanks to everyone who's asked, "How'd you get into my head?"

About the Author

Dawn Downey is the author of *Stumbling Toward the Buddha: Stories about Tripping over My Principles on the Road to Transformation.*

Book number three is in the works (*Searching for My Heart: Essays about Love*).

Her essays have been published by *River Blood and Corn, Shambhala Sun, Skirt! Magazine, Kansas City Voices: A Periodical of Writing and Art,* and *The Best Times.* She has earned awards from the Missouri Writers Guild, Oklahoma Writers Federation, Northern Colorado Writers, and the Santa Barbara Writers Conference.

When her fingers aren't blazing across the keyboard, you'll find the author in a yoga class or walking the track at the YMCA. She lives with her husband, Ben Worth, in Kansas City, where they feed their addiction to Bollywood movies.

If you enjoyed *From Dawn to Daylight,* sign up for her newsletter at DawnDowney.com/newsletter sign-up, to receive a monthly essay in your email inbox.

Connect online at:
- DawnDowney.com
- DawnDowneyBlog.com
- Goodreads.com
- Vimeo.com/dawndowney